A RIDGE PRESS BOOK · DISTRIBUTED BY POCKET BOOKS, INC.

THE
PRIVATE
WORLD
OF
PABLO
PICASSO

BY DAVID DOUGLAS DUNCAN

Editor: JERRY MASON
Art Director: ALBERT A. SQUILLACE
Editorial Coordinator: RUTH BIRNKRANT
Copy Editor: ELIZABETH HULING
Production: ALLIED GRAPHIC ARTS, INC.
Printing: R. R. DONNELLEY & SONS COMPANY

Prepared and produced by THE RIDGE PRESS
551 Fifth Avenue, N. Y. 17, N. Y.
© *Copyright 1958, David Douglas Duncan*
Library of Congress Catalog Card Number: 58-5423

INDEX

SECTION FIVE

SECTION SIX

Maybe this is the happiest house on earth.

It also is the studio of an artist who has flamboyantly reshaped our visual world. By thinking unconventionally and working with the simplest of materials—sometimes even with abandoned junk from the streets—he has brought about this transformation while staying at home, fermenting an explosive imagination in the volcano of his own inexhaustible energy. Adhering strictly to artistic laws of his own invention . . . yet championing absolute freedom of creative thought for others; a believer in communism's philosophy . . . and still a generous contributor to the Catholic Church; intensely interested in the latest news . . . but living in almost total isolation from the world around him: the man is one of history's most contradictory personalities and, from a distance, nearly as perplexing as a roomful of his portraits. Adored and zealously followed by some; maligned and ridiculed by others; rarely venturing beyond his gate; never seeking a market for his talents; his face, nonetheless, is known everywhere. The demand for his time is so enormous as to make him quite probably the highest-paid man alive. His recognition and success have had no equals in our century—possibly never.

Pablo Picasso lives here.

Curiously, while Picasso's infrequent appearances in public cause as much excitement as those of a movie star and his prolific output towers over the entire horizon of art like a personally produced Mt. Everest, his home life has been a matter for speculation and his habits as an artist have remained a career-long mystery. At various times he has been photographed while painting on glass, or translucent parchment, or even thin air. These films were competently handled and added significant highlights to the lore of the man, yet he himself regarded them only as complex exercises which challenged his craftsmanship. Also, they were fun. Almost everything else about Picasso was unknown. He lived and worked behind his fence, in a private world of his own.

This book was created by selecting a few hundred photographs from the more than 10,000 taken while I was Picasso's guest, during the seventy-fifth year of his life. I had cameras on him for more than three full months, literally for every waking hour of every day. No picture was ever arranged for my benefit, no hand ever raised to prevent my shooting. Each photograph was taken by existing light under precisely those conditions in which the Maestro works, and lives.

When I had finished I asked Picasso whether there were any pictures which he would prefer to have omitted from the book. He drew back as though I had struck him, and replied, "But how could you think such a thing! It is *your* book. They are as you see me . . . they are true!" So, the book traces the exact course of my visit—and it is true.

It all began three years ago, in the desert wilderness of western Afghanistan. A story assignment had taken me to that remote corner of Asia to photograph the crumbled remains of fortress-cities destroyed by Tamerlane. While there an engineer friend noticed my watchband, which is made of Greek coins of the Fourth Century B.C., and remarked that he had found several which were similar while poking through nearby ruins. He later gave them to me. Among them was a small, persimmon-colored stone, a carnelian. On its face was the image of a rooster, engraved there by someone during the time of Christ. Somehow, in its simplicity, it reminded me of other birds drawn by another artist, Picasso—whom I didn't know. I felt he might like to have it some day, so I dropped it in my pocket. There it remained until long after I had left Afghanistan and returned home, in Rome, where I had the little rooster-stone set into a ring.

A couple of weeks later, headed for another assignment in Morocco, I stopped at Cannes, on the French Riviera. I knew Picasso's home was nearby. It took time to learn his telephone number. His neighbors appreciated the value he placed on privacy. Finally connected with his villa, *La Californie,* I explained who I was, where I'd come from, that I wished to leave the ring without bothering Picasso, and apologized for phoning without an introduction—that our only mutual friend had been photographer Bob Capa, killed a year earlier in Indochina. The soft voice on the phone asked me to wait a moment, then returned, and invited me to the house. It was Jacqueline Roque, the gentle, gracious girl who shares Picasso's life . . . who has dedicated hers to him.

The book began that day, as the monumental, wrought-iron gate of the villa swung open. I was face to face with a world so incredibly remote from the tourist traffic of Cannes that it could well have been a bridge to another planet.

A bronze, never-blinking Amazonian goddess, six feet tall, paired with a whimsically wind-blown, acetylene-welded fighting cock, guarded the front door. Picasso's massive boxer dog, Yan, lay sprawled across the marble steps between them. Inside, the front hall of the place was a jungle overflowing with mammoth tropical flowers, roosters, a mother ape tenderly carrying her young, bulging-eyed harpies, a very pregnant woman and a lyrically beautiful nude girl presented as a vase, cast in bronze like everything else. Unopened crates lined the walls. They held paintings returned from worldwide exhibitions, which Picasso had never troubled to unpack. Freshly painted ceramic plates, separated by old newspapers, were stacked upon the crates awaiting a trip to the firing kilns. I was led upstairs.

The second-floor salon was completely empty, except for a gigantic clothes closet—and a tethered goat. Two more doors and I met Pablo Picasso, in the bathtub.

And, I met Jacqueline.

Something extremely precious and rare was born in those few minutes of our first meeting. We three became friends, for life. It was that simple.

As the months passed, then a year, and I had long finished the assignment in Morocco, and others in Egypt and Ireland and Russia, I always stopped at *La Californie* when driving through Cannes. Each time, as I expressed delight over the ever-deepening tangle cluttering the floors, and enthusiasm for the story I saw there, Picasso invariably answered in his guttural Spanish, "This is your home . . . start today!" Last winter, coming back from the Austro-Hungarian border, I again stopped to see the Maestro and Jacqueline—and again there came his invitation.

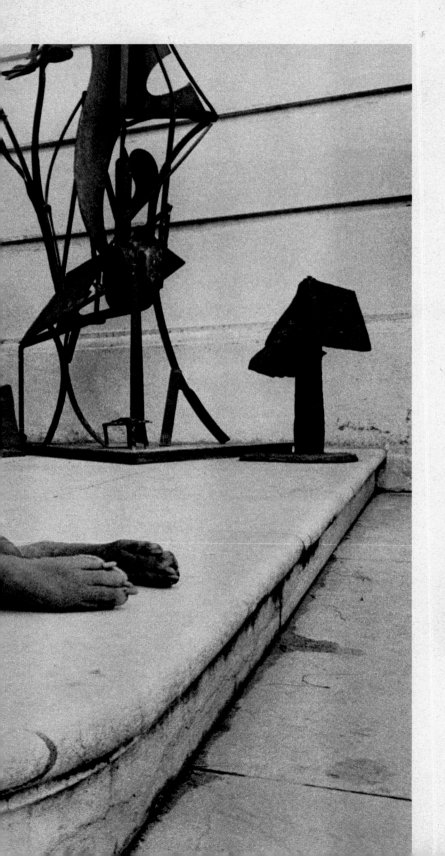

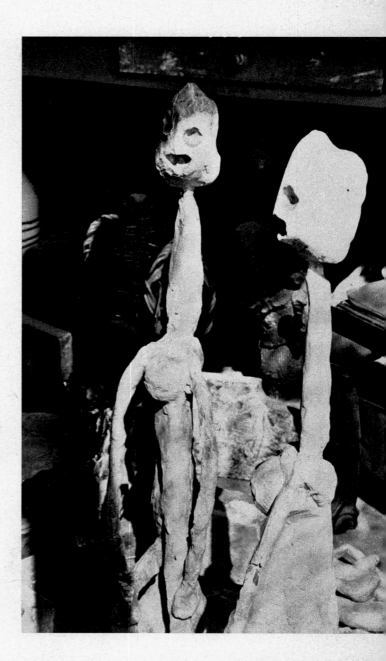

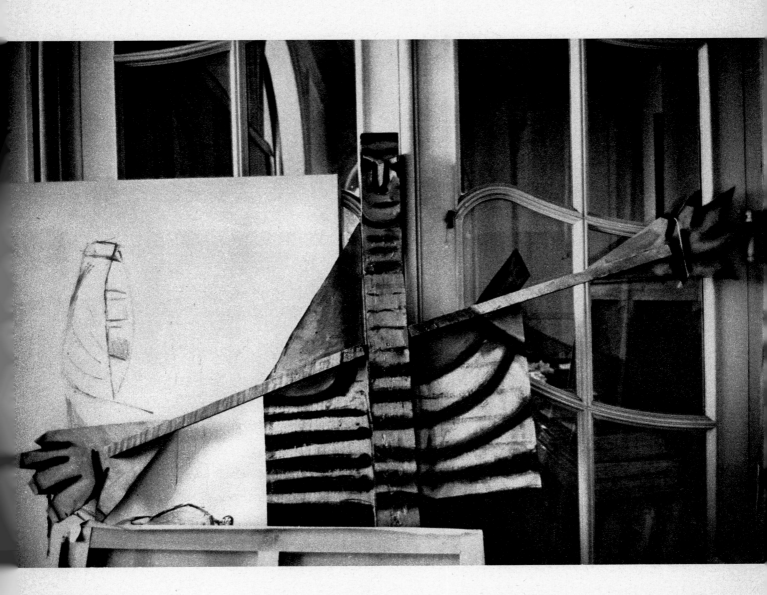

Life around *La Californie* was a joy in springtime. Sparkling Mediterranean sunlight poured down over the house, and upon the fantastic collection of creatures gathered behind it. There—in darkening sculpture—a proud and preposterously pregnant mother goat, a horrendous pagan-island sorceress, and the haughty daughter of an emperor met in silent company along the garden's edge, as though paying homage at a royal court. The pet nannygoat of the house, often tied to her sagging, metallic sister, was blissful. She devoured every flower within reach. No noise filtered through the garden from the town below. The great window-doors of the studio generally remained closed until noon; since Picasso spent most of his nights working, he liked to sleep late. Small songbirds and an occasional butterfly wandered out from the forested inner depths of the casually tended garden. Nothing had a sense of urgency. It was a peaceful place.

Late one morning, while changing lenses on the studio steps, I heard a sharp, curious sound among the trees. Seeing nothing, I had turned back to my cameras when it came again. My interest really aroused, I stepped away from the house and looked up—in time to see an exuberant Picasso on his bedroom balcony, twirling and shaking, heels pounding, palms cracking, dancing in the midday sun—dressed in Jacqueline's petticoat and an ancient African war helmet. It lasted but a moment. Then, jolting to an abrupt halt, he gripped the balcony's railing, looked off into the trees, and could be heard growling, almost belligerently, "Que bueno. Que BUENO!" "How good. How GOOD!," surely speaking of the beautiful day—and posting warning that he intended twisting *something* into unheard-of shapes before nightfall.

Children loved the weirdly wonderful inhabitants of the garden. Kathy—whose mother, Jacqueline, and father had separated years before in French West Africa—rarely passed the expectant old she-goat without leaping aboard, gouging her sandals into those poor bursting ribs. She was much too young a child to understand their meaning. Kathy's closest friend, Martine, spun her longest daydreams while swinging on her elbows between the witch and the princess. My own favorite place was a corner of the garden where I could sit deep among the trees, looking straight into the eyes of a Botticellian Venus—a classically majestic head, tilted inquisitively to one side as though listening to the forest sounds around her . . . serenity in bronze . . . decapitated and stuck in the birdbath by Picasso.

Probably no visitor to Picasso's home ever found more adventure there than did Lump, the dachshund puppy who was making his first trip out into the world with me. Lump had known nothing but a pampered existence in a Roman apartment as he grew into doghood.

Perhaps Lump's greatest thrill came the first morning he followed me into the garden. He had been chasing bees, in grass nearly as tall as himself, when he suddenly realized he was nose-to-nose with no bee. He had nearly run into the grazing goat, tied that morning to Picasso's monolithic statue "Shepherd Carrying a Lamb." At first Lump only stared, horrified. Then, crawling closer for a better look, he lay rigid on his belly with nostrils quivering, his unbelieving eyes almost bursting from his head. His lips trembled but he was much too scared to bark. He and the goat faced each other from about a yard apart. The tension exploded! Lump lurched backward, ears straight out, stubby little legs actually tripping themselves as he tumbled behind me for protection—and kept right on going. The goat hadn't moved a muscle.

Lump tore through the studio doors and into the dining room where Picasso and Jacqueline were starting their lunch. There he skidded to a stop. Within seconds he was at Picasso's knee, then in his lap, where the Maestro cradled the puppy, letting him find security in his arms. Jacqueline was astonished, because Picasso had displayed no affection for any dog in years. The big boxer, Yan, once belonged to another house and another era of the artist's life. Now, he just good-naturedly guarded the front door. With Lump it was different. It was mutual love at first sight. With scarcely a regretful backward glance, he had chosen a new home for himself.

One day, shortly after Lump had moved in to stay, we were well along with lunch when Picasso did an ordinary thing—in a most unordinary way. He had eaten his *sole Meunière*. Then, apparently on second thought, he picked the remains up and began gnawing on the bones of the intact skeleton almost as though he were playing a harmonica. I had never before seen a fish dispatched with such infinite precision or attention to the last hidden morsel. There was also a strangely pensive look on Picasso's face which made me react automatically. I had time for but a single shot before he jumped from the table, disappeared into the front of the villa—fishbone and all— and returned with a slab of moist potter's clay.

Shoving aside his plate, he carefully arranged the skeleton on the clay. Two sheets of sketching paper went over the bones, which the Maestro then began gently pressing into the soft clay. Once the skeleton was firmly embedded he tugged it free, repeating the process several times. He was making his own fossils.

He went again to the front of the house, this time returning with a large unpainted plate which he painstakingly covered with dull designs. Turning it over, he used his pocketknife to carve several more, equally simple, patterns on its base. Passing the table, where he had left his "fossils," he whipped the knife blade around the edge of the skeletal imprints until each fell free from the rough slab of clay. Two of these severely elegant fillets were then pressed into the decorated, but dismal, face of the plate. He sat back to look at his handiwork—slowly turning his potter's wheel. At that exact moment he looked up, and clearly read the question which must have filled my eyes. He chuckled, "Don't worry, Dooncan, those colors will all change in the fire up at the kiln. This will be emerald. That will be blue. But won't these fish be surprised when they discover they've lost their bodies somewhere?"

Occasionally Picasso sat absolutely still, while patches of brooding thoughtfulness swept across his sky—but never for long. That fish plate was made during a period of intense ceramic activity when the studio overflowed with eagles and owls and fauns and fighting bulls and lopsided clowns. Janot, the driver, was kept busy each morning gingerly hauling the fragile creations to the kilns of Vallauris, the village above Cannes where Picasso's ceramics have always been fired. Picasso never seemed to tire, nor to exhaust his imagination. No two plates were the same, and the Maestro worked far into the night, every night, dreaming of and painting new ones.

When I first began covering the life at *La Californie,* I would arrive early each morning in order to thoroughly familiarize myself with its gardens and sculptures, while waiting for Picasso to awaken. There was much to see and to learn. No one had ever before been given such freedom around his home. I wanted to make the most of it. Jacqueline came downstairs fairly early, but she was busy getting Kathy off to school and making arrangements for running the villa, so I saw little of her except as she hurried in and out of the house on her errands. After Picasso came down and opened the studio—a ritual he himself always performed with a huge key tied by an old string to his belt—I had the three great rooms to myself while he examined work done the night before. During that year when he kept offering me the story which I saw around the villa, he had always said that it was my home. He meant it.

There was but one Great Law in that house: DO NOT MOVE ANYTHING! Everything had its place and even its own dust pattern. To move anything out of its place, or pattern, might easily destroy a composition, unseen by anyone else, which Picasso had been watching, thinking about, and turning into other forms in his mind. It had to be remembered, constantly, that the house and garden constituted almost the entire physical world seen by Picasso, and that he was terribly dependent upon them in many ways.

Delightfully, this law did not apply to children or to animals. In Picasso's world children were born to run free. If a child moved things, even canvases themselves, he would say only "Good... Good!" or "How droll!," and nothing more, apparently having already accepted the compositional changes as the functioning of a law greater than any of his own. During all of the months that I was a guest at the villa, while Kathy and her friend Martine and, later, other children played endlessly—and Lump and Yan and the goat frolicked all around the place—I never heard the word "Don't" nor saw a child or pet punished . . . and nothing was ever broken.

Picasso's affection for birds and animals has been traced back almost three-quarters of a century. As a child in Malaga, on the south coast of Spain, he often carried pigeons to school as pets which he sketched, having borrowed them from his tolerant artist father—who was using them as models in his own conventional paintings. Today, *La Californie's* most sweeping view of the Mediterranean, and the sky beyond, is enjoyed from the third-floor balcony where Picasso's pigeons live.

Although remote from the activities of the town below them, Picasso and Jacqueline had very few hours when they were alone together. For a telephone number that had been difficult to track down, it appeared as though the line was always busy with greetings, or requests for visits, from book publishers, art dealers, bullfighters, museum directors, movie stars, or old friends like Jaime Sabartés, a crony since their youth in Barcelona. Picasso was genuinely pleased when people tried to call him. A surprisingly gregarious man for one who seemed to seek seclusion, he would have enjoyed seeing everyone, but this would have made work quite impossible. Thus Jacqueline took the calls and at times, very diplomatically, expressed Picasso's regrets: he was painting. She relayed the messages, but only he made those decisions.

One old acquaintance for whom the gate always opened immediately was poet-musician Jean Cocteau, who lived nearby on the Côte d'Azur. Picasso had first designed stage sets for a Cocteau ballet in Rome, nearly forty years earlier. Their friendship continued through the decades into the present era at the villa.

It was during a Cocteau visit that I first glimpsed another sparkling side of Picasso. Jacqueline had dashed to answer the door, leaving Picasso in the garden where they had been walking.

Cocteau was ushered into the studio. Picasso had disappeared. I was beginning to notice how strange it was when CRASH! Picasso leaped from behind some canvases masked as an Italian clown, shouting "Que bella Roma . . . bella Roma!" and grinning happily, with false nose and mustache askew, his eyes flashingly fixed on his guest.

A few minutes later Picasso doffed the disguise and was thumping out a never-heard-before tune on a battered old African marimba which, like unnumbered thousands of other seemingly unrelated curiosities, had been shoved into a corner of the studio. Surprisingly, although Picasso came from music-loving Spain, and though he had been a friend of Ravel and had worked with Stravinsky in Paris earlier in his life, he never displayed the slightest interest in music during the months I was making photographs around the villa.

Thus, it was a real surprise to see him hammer out a tune on the marimba, a tune certainly of his own imagination. He managed to play it twice. Then he handed the sticks to musician Cocteau—bandmaster to backward pupil—to see what *he* could get out of the instrument. Cocteau had only begun developing the throbbing vibrations of a professionally played marimba when Picasso chortled, "Ah HA! Just as I suspected. No music in you at ALL!" Whereupon Cocteau threw all restraint aside and began beating the bark off the quivering instrument. He filled the studio with the staccato song of Picasso while the beaming composer at his shoulder delightedly kept interrupting with, "That's better—*much* better!"

Cocteau had been gone but a moment when Picasso turned to the most immediate commitment on hand. He began pulling canvases out of a corner, selecting portraits to be loaned to America for a series of tremendous retrospective exhibitions of his work scheduled in New York, Chicago and Philadelphia. His most recent bronze statues loomed starkly over him as he flipped through the paintings. An inestimable fortune in portraits flashed into the open, then immediately disappeared, as he dragged out, glanced at, and made his decision on several dozen canvases. Many were of Jacqueline: first as an almond-eyed Turkish bride; then as a swan-necked sphinx; finally, wearing a black scarf and a black sweater, simply as Jacqueline. While Picasso stood motionless for a moment behind the last painting, with his own somber eyes burning back into mine, I wondered what he was thinking, for that tranquil, poetically idealized image had never before been photographed—nor seen outside of his studio.

There was also a charcoal drawing of Jacqueline which the Maestro had later dressed in gold and gray brocade—the wrapper from a candy box. And there was one of the most famous Picassos of recent years, of the child Sylvette with her pony-tail hair bouncing on her shoulders. Other paintings were spun out and away again before I had more than glanced at them. The last one was the incredibly innocent-eyed portrait of his son, Paul, dressed as a clown. Painted more than thirty years ago, it became one of the most loved portraits in art.

His rummaging finished, the private Picasso show ended as abruptly as it had begun. He chose the portraits of Jacqueline as the Sphinx and Paul as a clown, to join nearly forty other canvases being sent to the United States.

Later that afternoon he stood in the front doorway watching his paintings being hauled out through the rain into an old truck, to begin their journey to lands he had never seen.

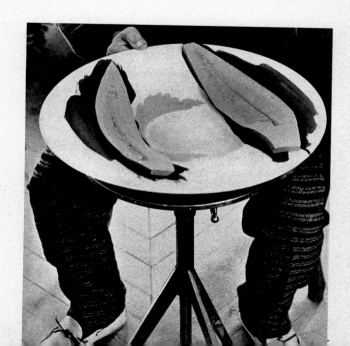

There were days at the villa when Picasso seemed to be the most homesick man in the world.

Ever since 1938, when Generalissimo Francisco Franco's fascist Falangistas won the Spanish Civil War, republican Pablo Picasso had boycotted his homeland. Surely, the spiritual price he paid was enormous. Few Spaniards could ever have been more typically Spanish than the Maestro. It showed in every way: in the utter simplicity and honest warmth of his hospitality . . . in his deep attachment for the roof that sheltered him . . . in the unfailing grace with which he dealt with people who, not infrequently, tried to impose upon him . . . in his legs which seemed to root from the land itself . . . in his impractical stand on some issues, where he sided with the underdogs simply because of their emotional appeal . . . in his fanatical love for the place of his birth, which he shunned, nevertheless, in rock-stubborn pride—his only way of expressing ever-lasting opposition to the ruling regime in Madrid.

Picasso's longing for Spain could actually be seen only when he swirled a great bullfighter's cloak over his shoulders, after adjusting with infinite care a stiff-brimmed Cordoban hat on his head. Then he would enmesh Jacqueline in the ivory folds of a shimmering Sevillian mantilla. In his heart he was going home—for a moment. But it was terrible, at that time, to look into his eyes.

Other days, and they were the vast majority, Picasso's natural gaiety filled the house. This was especially true while visitors were in *La Californie*. On those occasions Picasso was totally aware of every individual around him, like Easter morning when the ceramist Ramie brought his family down from Vallauris to pay their respects. The Ramies had been in the studio but a moment when Picasso noticed that their youngest son, Alain, was ill at ease and looked lost. Immediately turning away from the group he crossed the room to return with the bullfighter's cloak and Cordoban hat—perhaps his most treasured personal possessions—which he casually fitted upon the youth. Stepping back and seeing the boy's radiant face, he then added delight to happiness by quickly slipping into his clown's disguise and confiding to Alain, ''We'll be partners! We'll go out into the world. We'll join the circus, or the *Folies Bergère,* or the movies — and make a thousand million francs!''

It was that same Easter Sunday when I first discovered there was one minor art which Picasso had never mastered. Jacqueline had spent hours in the kitchen that morning helping France, her part-time maid, to prepare a real holiday banquet. Their most loving efforts went into charcoal-broiling a chicken and stuffing it with almonds. Picasso took one pleased look at the production when it appeared, then, growling his all-inclusive "How droll!," speared the bird onto his own plate, where he carved it. That chicken could have been carved just about as daintily—and just as fast—by stuffing it with a hand grenade.

The following week the dining room was again the scene of great activity, but of an entirely different nature. Yves Montand, the French movie star, with his actress-wife Simone Signoret, had dropped by to see the Maestro. There they ran into a newspaper correspondent named Georges Tabaraud, who had come, with his wife and daughter, to interview Picasso. All four, Picasso, Montand, Signoret and Tabaraud, were reportedly members of the French Communist Party—but with a considerable difference between them. The year before, together with other French writers, actors and artists, Picasso, Montand and his wife had signed an open letter of protest to the Party following the Soviet Army's stamping out of the Hungarian revolution. Now, while Lump and Yan skirmished all over the floor and into the Maestro's drawings, Montand faced Tabaraud—who was representing *Le Patriote,* one of the official French Communist newspapers. Montand's protest of the Red Army's intervention was as blistering as had been the open letter. Tabaraud countered with the Party's clichés—that the revolution, in reality, had been a capitalist-inspired counter-revolutionary uprising. Montand threw sarcasm and well-documented facts into the argument. Tabaraud defended his position as best he could. The flare-up lasted nearly an hour. Picasso contributed only one thing to the entire episode—the flickering cross fire of his eyes, which pinpointed one man, then the other. He added nothing else whatsoever—literally, not one word.

In a far corner of the room a child had fallen under *La Californie's* spell. Tabaraud's daughter, Marie-Christine, oblivious to the discussion swirling above her head, was on her knees crawling among owls and goblins and tiger cats — through a wondrous world of make-believe. Veteran Lump was stretched out in Picasso's broken-down old chair, acting like the keeper of the keys and languidly bidding her enter. The little girl had just embarked upon her exploration when she was dragged away to lunch. Picasso, instantly sensing her disappointment, left the table and reappeared immediately as the genial king of clowns offering the eight-year-old his castle. From that moment she was free to prowl unrestrained into a magician's maze . . . to be her own Alice in Wonderland . . . to dream a child's dreams, alone.

Another afternoon some visitors asked who I was. Picasso simply handed them a book that I had done on the Korean War—a book of anguish, for it showed U.S. Marines dying under enemy fire. As the callers turned the pages I kept a telephoto lens on Picasso. He seemed unable to look back into the faces of the wounded, or of the dying. When he reached the photograph of a friend of mine, sprawled dead on a hilltop, he buckled as though he himself had been shot.

My war pictures seemed to crush Picasso. His eyes dimmed with total compassion for what he had just seen. It was the most tragic face I had ever photographed.

So the weeks rolled by at *La Californie,* with each day different from the one before . . . and different from the one to follow. There was the evening the doctor called to give Picasso his periodic check-up. It appeared so unnecessary that I was surprised. No man spared himself less than Picasso as he hurried up and down the villa's stairs, or dragged massive sculptures and canvases through the studio, or chased the dogs or goat away from his work, or cavorted lightheartedly with Jacqueline or their guests. A rhinoceros would have had as much need for a doctor, yet Picasso believed it was a good idea . . . so the medic was called. Apparently the results were always the same—the Maestro should have been examining the doctor. But Picasso, the prudent Spaniard, had it figured still another way. While the doctor was in the villa he had Kathy checked over, too, with an injection thrown in for good measure.

The doctor's professional interest in Picasso was probably matched by his personal curiosity about the Maestro's somewhat bizarre tweed trousers with their glaring black and white horizontal stripes. We who were around the villa daily thought nothing of them, in fact they were even on the conservative side—compared with others he was saving upstairs. But strangers visiting the house for the first time, or old-timers who had been away for a while, were usually stopped absolutely cold when Picasso would first appear in those pants—especially if it happened in the garden where the sun hit the pattern full strength. Picasso's answer was always a beaming "Droll, no?," then an explanation.

"All my life I was forced to buy pants with stripes running this way [up-and-down chopping motions with his hands]. The shops offered nothing else. Yet, all that time I wanted pants with stripes running like this [hands slicing sideways]. Well, looking through an old book one day, I saw a self-portrait by Courbet . . . *he* had on pants with stripes right across the bottom. So I called Sapone over from his tailor shop in Nice. He brought everything he had. It took time— but we found it! No, no, he didn't make the checkered socks. They're English. They're ordinary! Droll, these stripes, no?"

Another sporadic visitor to the house was Arrias, the Spanish barber from Vallauris. He always came at nightfall. Picasso's haircut was welcomed by both, for it gave them a chance to revert to their mother tongue. They never mentioned ceramics or paintings or Vallauris or Cannes: they spoke of *veronicas* and *mariposas, muletas* and *espadas*. They spoke of *la corrida*—the bull-fight. The haircut itself was a casual affair where Picasso switched on his big studio painting lights and Arrias dragged a chair in among the bronzes and canvases. One night the spell of the house gripped Arrias, too. He had just finished clipping and sweeping off the dome of the Maestro's head. Picasso had jumped up to talk with Jacqueline when, with a snort and a roar and a pawing of feet, Arrias grabbed up the empty chair, slapped its hornlike legs over his head —and charged. *La corrida* had come home!

Quiet came late to *La Californie* on those days when its visitors seemed determined to stay for-ever. Sometimes it was heartbreaking to watch the wasted hours flow by, thinking what those idle hands might have been shaping in the meantime. But Picasso was always the attentive and generous host, who never, even obliquely, tried to start his most tenacious guest toward the door. One day, after an old-timer had knocked at lunch time, then stayed on through the afternoon and into the early evening, Picasso passed me at the opposite end of the studio. I made a pointed observation about the unbelievable lack of understanding in a person who could so waste another man's time. Picasso stopped and looked at me for a moment, then replied very quietly. "No, no, Dooncan. *Never* think like that! Remember, he is my friend—and it's only a life."

When at last alone, with the house gathering its stillness around him, he would generally turn on the lamps in the dining room and read the evening paper. It was such a commonplace act that it always struck me as surprising, possibly because at that moment he could have been any of a multitude of men who were doing exactly the same thing—if one overlooked the gigantic bronze head on the cluttered mantelpiece, and the black and white horizontally striped pants, and the waiting potter's wheel . . . and the almost visible, absolute silence which surrounded him while he concentrated on the news.

Still later, after a frugal meal of raw vegetables and bread and cheese—often precariously bal-anced on his potter's wheel—Picasso went to work. Jacqueline read in the old broken-down chair behind him. Kathy and Lump and Yan and the goat and the pigeons would all be asleep in various parts of the house . . . and Picasso would work. He would often work without a break of any kind right into the dawning hours of morning. Those were the hours in which he created paintings, or woodcuts, or engravings, or sculptures, or etchings, or ceramics, or almost anything. Long after midnight one night, while watching him place the last painted plate of an almost endless series on the packing crates in the front-hall corridor—with the single light bulb barely outlin-ing his head, and cigarette, and the plate against the darkness—I remembered a line I had once read in Khalil Gibran's *The Prophet,* where he wrote "Work is Love made visible" . . . and I thought that it might easily have been dedicated to the tireless man in *La Californie.*

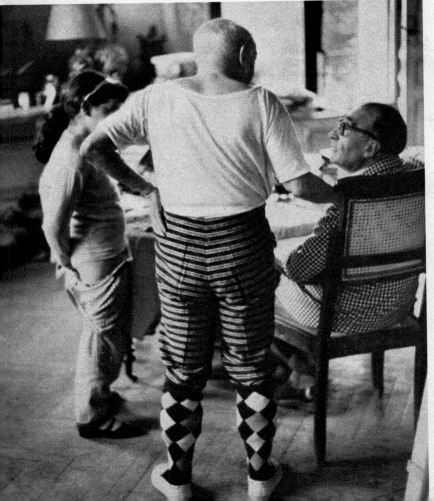

Very few events lured Picasso away from *La Californie*. He shunned every invitation to cultural or political functions and rarely attended even the ceremonies inaugurating exhibitions of his own work. But there was *one* great exhibition, and for it he dropped everything. It was the bullfight in Arles, that southern French town whose scorching sun had been glorified by—while probably killing—another painter, named Vincent van Gogh.

He tried to attend at least one of these *corridas* each year. For everyone else around the villa his expeditionary preparations were sufficient excitement and *corrida* unto themselves. The Maestro would go stamping through the house ready to leave, come to a dead stop at the front door, disappear into the studio, then reappear later casually wondering what had caused the delay. He was not being temperamental. He was just heartily squeezing the final tasty juices out of every aspect of his trip—exactly as he did from painting, and from life itself.

The Spanish community of Arles received Picasso like a legendary king. When he strolled arm-in-arm with Jacqueline through the town a whole retinue of admirers choked the street behind them. His strapping 37-year-old son, Paul, whose childhood portraits had touched millions of hearts, came from Paris to walk beside him. As they started for the arena, hard-eyed, silent strangers materialized from nowhere to escort the Maestro through the crowds. He was made patron of honor of many *corridas*. In response, Picasso, who loathed being trapped in conventional clothing and who loved his black and white striped pants and rough fisherman's shirt, wore a dark blue business suit, white shirt and a necktie . . . his highest tribute to any occasion. No one in Arles could have guessed what that gesture cost him.

During the bullfight itself—all fluttering banners and trumpeting pageantry . . . agonized horses, poised banderillas, swirling capes and wild hysteria . . . an eerie silence . . . a breathless moment . . . then death—Picasso sat motionless, hands at his sides, unspeaking, alone. It was impossible to see his face. But without any doubt whatsoever he had only the bull and the matador mirrored in his eyes. He took no side. He was the absolute spectator.

After the visit to Arles the only indication that Picasso had been away was his playfully twirling his bath towel like a matador's cape and trying to provoke charges from across Jacqueline's and Kathy's second-floor sitting room. He was again soon comfortable in his striped pants and often on the telephone calling his old friend Jaime Sabartés, in Paris, cajoling him to drop everything, to come immediately to *La Californie*.

Compared to Picasso, Sabartés was the opposite face of the Spanish coin. His whole existence flowed as a gently meandering brook into the cascading torrent which was the Maestro's life. For years he had served as Picasso's self-appointed chronicler and business secretary. It was his way of expressing admiration and affection for the man he had known since the end of the last century. The shy Barcelonan was an undemonstrative man who was always conservatively dressed. His dry, monosyllabic remarks sometimes ended all tableside discussions. He was unswayed by the emotional attractions of any argument. Sabartés also brought wry humor into the house, plus a piercing talent for weighing his famous friend's work. Picasso appeared only to greet him, then headed back into his bedroom and was not seen again for two full days. No one seemed perturbed. However, the *corrida* was not even mentioned around the villa, which had acquired an atmosphere unfelt before. Meanwhile, another stranger had arrived, but he stayed in the basement all day.

One noon, four days after the bullfight, Picasso came trotting downstairs as though he had been gone but a moment. Jacqueline had explained earlier that he was perfectly well—he was just sitting in bed, thinking. Now, although rain was pouring down outside, he seemed oddly jubilant. Five of us, Picasso, Jacqueline, Sabartés, myself and the stranger from the basement, Jacques Frelaut, who I learned was a master printmaker from Montmartre, ate lunch in the kitchen that day. The dining-room table had been converted into a studio workbench before the trip to Arles.

The meal finished, Frelaut returned to the basement. Jacqueline curled into the broken-down old chair in the dining-room corner, her feet propped on a bronze tomcat. Sabartés half-dozed in his friend's rocking chair in the next room. And I stood at the Maestro's shoulder watching a truly great spectacle unfold. I saw Picasso paint the entire Spanish bullfight, from beginning bugle to the final fatal thrust.

In a period of exactly three hours he made the Arles *corrida* live again. He made all *corridas* live again. Dipping his slender brush into a dark solution of syrupy sugar, he painted on glistening copper plates. And as he painted I saw, once more, the prancing horse lead matadors and picadórs into the arena . . . the first charge of a fighting bull lunging from the chutes . . . the exquisite, almost feminine, footwork of the banderilleros as they danced seemingly suspended just off the horns of the bull . . . the undiminished dignity of the animal, even with his life ebbing away, when he still turned and warily faced his foe . . . then that dedicated moment of mourning, while the slender matador and his attendants stood their deathwatch around the stricken brute, sinking ever lower upon the sand before them.

There was no haste in the way Picasso painted. He simply began at the left and painted to the right. He was somewhat like a medieval scribe penning a romantic tale of the bullfight. But, instead of flowing words in ornate script, his were flashing swords and broken bodies and the poetry of violence in man. Few figures needed more than a stroke of the brush. No plate took more than a couple of minutes to complete. Once the brush lifted from the copper all painting on it was finished, forever.

There *was* one erasure. Picasso had just pushed a plate aside, a plate of frantic action, when he pulled it back, took his handkerchief and rubbed out the image of the matador. Looking up at me, but not really seeing me at all, he muttered, "He made a mistake!" He, *the matador,* had made a mistake. With that, Picasso repainted the man being flung skyward by the infuriated bull. He had indeed made a mistake! There was no question but that Picasso was totally submerged in the drama appearing on the plates before him, even though he was its author and controlled all of its action completely. He had painted a physical situation in which the matador could *only* get gored, regardless of Picasso—who immediately recognized its truth. The matador was killed. Then, the next bullfight began.

Only once did I see Picasso's eyes. It was for a reflected instant near the beginning when he tilted a mirror-smooth plate into the rainy afternoon light, to paint sturdy legs under the picadors' horses — with a flick of his brush.

Picasso's face was a rigid mask when he painted. Yet the brush itself, pulsating up and down like a great phonograph needle, seemed to be connected directly with something vibrating deep within the man. There was little more to be seen—without looking at the copper plates.

After painting the last plate Picasso went straight to the basement. The place was a labyrinth of cell-like storerooms, all but one of them empty. That exception was exciting. It was a printing plant. Picasso had moved in his own engraver's press when he bought *La Californie*. Jacques Frelaut had been quietly cleaning and balancing its rollers and pressure-plate. All was ready when Picasso padded down the stairs in his soft Moroccan slippers.

He again picked up a slender brush. Again he faced the highly polished copper with a sticky, molasses-colored solution—this time concentrated perchloride of iron. He was making aquatints, etching away the sugar images, following a process rarely attempted any more because of the tedious labor and feather touch required of the artist.

Jacqueline sat on an empty box, waiting. She waited, watching Picasso at his work. She waited with a look in her eyes such as few men could arouse in a woman, or, once aroused, few could keep alive. It was a look of love so profound that had it been seen in an artist's studio during the epic age of Renaissance painters and poets it would have been the heart of a song, or a verse —and it would still be known today.

Jacqueline was waiting for Picasso, so Lump waited, too. It was late and he was a sleepy little dog, but he waited with Jacqueline—as best he could.

Hours rushed by. No one had eaten. At dusk Sabartés had come down from the studio where he had been reading. There was no thought of interrupting work on the etchings until Frelaut had inked the first plate and pulled a print. All eyes followed the sweeping arc of the handles as Freulaut spun the press. I was surprised when the print appeared. No one said anything. There was not a sound. Then I understood: these were professionals. Four pairs of eyes were cutting across every inch of that etching. The anticipated outburst of comment came at last—just a low rustling of voices barely audible across the room.

Picasso and Frelaut went back to work with scarcely a word exchanged. Picasso etched other plates. Frelaut washed and inked them, and ran them through the press. Then he leaned patiently on the table while Picasso minutely probed each print under an engraver's magnifying glass. The Maestro seemed capable of working right on through the night. Sabartés napped in a corner. Jacqueline had gone up to the kitchen to prepare supper, which we ate long after midnight. Lump was fast asleep in the broken-down chair out in the darkened studio. It was typical of many, many nights at *La Californie*.

The next day at lunch, after thinking constantly of the sheer visual power displayed by Picasso in memorizing, then painting and etching those bullfight scenes, I turned for another really good look into his eyes. And there they were, as always before—the sometimes merry, other times somber, but most often quizzically unblinking chestnut orbs reaching out to lasso everything sharing this life around him.

Lunch was always great fun at *La Californie,* but especially when we moved into the kitchen to eat. It was the major meal of the day. There were dishes from many lands, and in great abundance. Guests like Sabartés and Frelaut often had their choice of Spanish *chorizo,* Norwegian smoked salmon, Dutch smoked eel or Italian anchovies; French, Italian or Spanish wines; Mediterranean mullet, Casablancan couscous, Chinese chow mein or Bavarian roasts; home-grown vegetables; endive, lettuce or watercress salads; Camembert, Roquefort, Edam or Stilton cheeses; Malaga raisins, African bananas, Spanish melons, local grapes or berries; American cashew nuts, Swiss pralines or Austrian chocolates, and French coffee. Jacqueline and Picasso served one of the most cosmopolitan tables in Europe, yet the rarest thing of all was its simple informality.

Meals were family-style, served first by the Maestro from the head of the table. Then Jacqueline generally took over. Even before a plate was empty Picasso was lustily forcing second, even third helpings upon their guests. Nothing could be refused without offending his Spanish hospitality. But if one watched Picasso, a curious trait was revealed. He took almost nothing! While the others were happily devouring a gastronomic map of the world, he ate raw mushrooms with plain white rice, a bit of unsalted meat or fish, a leaf or two of lettuce without salad dressing— washing it all down with half a glass of fresh spring water from the Alps. He left nothing on his plate. He sometimes sipped light wine, but only on the most important occasions. His greatest treat was chocolate ice cream. He ate less than Lump, yet he developed enough energy for an Olympic track team—and he was almost as active.

Picasso's breakfast was even simpler than his lunches. When he woke up in mid-morning he had only a little coffee in hot milk, and a piece of bread. After that he would drowse again, or read his mail, or play with Lump, who by that time was often lying right beside him on the pillow, peering into his face, just waiting for permission to wriggle under the sheets, too.

The bedroom, like the rest of the house, was undoubtedly unique on the face of this earth. It had to be mounted like a horse, not entered! For its daily cleaning Jacqueline must have resorted to voodoo. Books, magazines, newspapers, bushels of letters, bronzes, lithographs, candlesticks, a chamber pot, African helmets, crayon drawings of summer flowers, Lump's sleeping basket and much-chewed blanket, Italian sandals, Moroccan slippers, Norwegian sweaters, Navajo moccasins, Spanish shirts, Irish scarfs and a bottle of French mineral water were among the things stacked shoulder-high against the walls—or hanging on them. There was one collapsing overstuffed chair near the huge French-door window which opened onto the garden. Picasso's socks, undershirt, shorts, shirt and pants were piled on the chair in the summer's sun, or on the radiator in winter. A rug of his own design covered part of the floor.

Then there was the bed! It was low, square and enormous. It was covered with a magnificent Chilean vicuña quilt whose silken fur was everyone's delight, including Lump's. Picasso's breakfast tray battled for space with the papers and mail and telegrams and samples of ceramics still dusty from the kiln. The area immediately surrounding the bed served as *La Californie's* biggest ash tray—although there were times when Picasso rose to the challenge presented by the chamber pot in the fireplace across the room. He rarely hit it! He periodically observed that he must remember to use the regular ash tray which Jacqueline always placed beside him—especially when he speculated on the acrobatics that might be required to get out of the room if a glowing cigarette should land in the inflammable forest surrounding him. But those gloomily pessimistic restraints soon vanished. He would lean back with another cigarette in his hand, and read or only think, while resting against the unvarnished headboard of his bed. Notes and phone numbers were scribbled on the planking. Its shape suited the rest of the bed surprisingly well—considering the fact that it was the back of a tremendous oil painting which the Maestro had dragged up from the studio and propped against the wall.

While Picasso painted and Jacqueline devoted all of her efforts to making *La Californie* a gay, warm home, freckle-faced Kathy's days were filled with school and homework. I saw her mostly on Thursdays and Sundays, French children's holidays from classes. On those days she was everywhere . . . in the garden climbing among the sculptures, on the driveway playing hopscotch, upstairs confiding to her mother and whispering to Lump, or finding gifts—like a single rose from the yard—to give to the Maestro when he was not busy making something. Among the handful of people in the world who called Picasso "Pablo," she was the only one to call him "Pablito"—the Spanish language's affectionate diminutive. Her friend, Martine, practically lived at the villa. During all the months I was around the house I never saw them play with dolls.

No interruptions of any kind were tolerated by Jacqueline once Picasso began to work. She sat in the broken-down old chair in the dining room, or on the garden steps in the sun. The doors to the kitchen and through the front of the house were closed and often locked. The back-hall telephone—the only one on the first floor—was turned off. The garden doors remained open, but Lump alone might enter. *La Californie's* master was insulated from all the world except that of his own mind.

The studio had always been the holiest place in Picasso's world. No outsider had ever stayed there when he lifted his brushes. He never actually gave me permission either. During the first several weeks of my visit he would come over to me after lunch and say, with a friendly whack on the shoulder, "Pués, ahora a trabajar. Al camino, Gitano" . . . "Well, now to work. To the road, Gypsy." From the very beginning we both had understood his invitation to mean that I was free to photograph only around the villa and its gardens, but nothing while he worked. That was a journalistically, world-renowned taboo. I was still getting far more than anyone else had been offered. I was elated. Then, one afternoon as I was preparing to leave, he brushed by me while hurrying to the front of the house. He returned with an unpainted plate. After arranging his colors in front of himself his eyes snapped up into mine—then went down again to the plate. Not a word was exchanged. But never again did I hit the road to my hotel until it was everyone's bedtime . . . and Picasso's work for the day finished.

Nothing ever dimmed the novelty of watching Picasso working at the end of the path across the studio floor. He seemed to be always leaning over the dinner table or his potter's wheel, oblivious to everything around him. My camera was at his side for so many hundreds of hours that it became a completely familiar member of the household. We rarely talked. I almost never asked a question. Jacqueline helped me later if there were uncertainties to be clarified. Picasso would have answered immediately had he ever known I was perplexed by anything in his studio. But the very last thing I desired was to make him aware of another person in the room who *might* be wondering what was happening to the object in his hands.

Still, as the months passed and his boundless imagination carried him into many fields of art, his bass-fiddle voice sometimes rumbled out passing remarks, usually concerning his work. There was the afternoon when he stooped to collect his ceramics colors, hidden away in cherished fruit jars and old coffee cans. He chuckled, and said, ''This equipment looks like an amateur's. No! No! It's worse!''—and then proceeded to paint a whole series of plates having a market value of about $2,500 apiece. Another day, when it was raining, he looked at a faded photostat of one of his most famous etchings, done when he was a very young man. The scene was a musty café. An emaciated, destitute man sat with one arm draped protectively over the bone-thin shoulders of his wife. Their plates were empty. Their bottle empty. Their lives empty—except for each other. Someone, not Picasso, long ago titled it ''The Frugal Repast.'' Picasso told me that when he made the etching he tried to sell it to Paris art dealers for five francs (about $1) a copy, but found no buyer. He gave all the copies to friends. Several years ago a single print came into the market. It brought nearly $5,000 at auction.

Perhaps the weather reminded him of it, but he described another day when he had roamed the streets of Paris lugging an armload of canvases, trying to sell them at any price to the dealers. Even the bread on which he had been starving was gone. The dealers refused everything. It began to rain. Picasso asked several dealers whether he might just protect his work in their shops until the storm passed. They refused. Today, of course, those ''Blue Period'' paintings are among the most treasured exhibits in the world's greatest art museums and in homes where $100,000 pictures are hung.

Last year in Paris his dealer Kahnweiler exhibited and sold 70 canvases painted by Picasso the year before. Best-informed sources estimated that the sale brought an average of $15,000 a picture—somewhere around $1,000,000 for the lot.

The subject of picture prices almost never arose in my talks with Picasso. No work was ever sold at his studio; contact with the buying public was handled by his dealer. The nearest he ever came to mentioning art as a business was the evening he looked down at something he had been making and then nodded to himself. ''It's like a lottery. A man might win a lottery once in a lifetime. It's every day with Kahnweiler! Paintings . . . ceramics . . . etchings . . . bronzes, and all the rest. It's like winning the National Lottery—every day!'' Then he went on. ''Look, Gypsy, we can't eat fifty times a day. Prices really don't mean a thing! They sell for a thousand, or a million—it's all the same, now.'' However, Picasso was an extremely proud and shrewd Spaniard. He clearly remembered other days. He knew his market value and made very sure it stayed in the stratosphere—even though he couldn't eat those fifty meals a day. I was there when he did nothing more than sign his name on several hundred lithographs. It took about an hour. The fee was a flat $10,000.

Another time, art dealer Pierre Matisse brought an earlier-painted still life to the studio for his signature. The picture had been a gift from the Maestro to Henri Matisse, Pierre's father.

After Pierre left the villa with the canvas—autographed for nothing, of course—Picasso shrugged and observed, "Paintings are like personal checks . . . more negotiable when signed."

In looking at all of the paintings in *La Californie*, I never saw his name on a canvas. Many were pictures that had been exhibited around the world. "Of course not," Picasso grunted, "I know who did them." He then went back to carefully carving dancing fauns on tiles. He had started the day molding clay doves, switched to painting plates, then begun the tiles. I mentioned that he had already produced an interesting variety of things for one afternoon. He seemed to agree, then added, "Paintings . . . tiles . . . sculptures . . . back to painting. The combination is good—like salad." He apparently harbored no illusions that every canvas touched ended as a masterpiece, whether by his hand or that of any other artist. Sabartés once got him into a wonderfully candid after-dinner discourse on the relative merits of great-name modern painters. When he stopped for coffee, I asked him whom he considered the greatest painters of all time. He hardly missed a gulp while answering, "It depended upon the day."

Picasso's feelings for his pictures were exceedingly paternal—so long as they remained unframed. For him a painting was very much alive and still subject to possible changes, until it went under glass. Then it was finished. Finished in the sense that he lost almost all interest in it. It was beyond the touch of his fingertips, beyond his brush. It had been ornately entombed.

Probably few men have more openly radiated their shining love affair with life than Picasso. His harmony with his earth and its creatures was a phenomenon which he wore easily, like his Spanish cloak. Other men felt it, too. But with animals it was incredibly noticeable. Lump became Picasso's devoted little sputnik at their first meeting. The nannygoat remained on her belly munching leaves if any of the rest of us walked by. When Picasso passed she clattered to her feet, straining to be seen and caressed. During his few trips into the countryside, dogs never barked at him. One evening, when the studio lights were blazing and the garden door open, a bat flew into the house. It circled a couple of times—then swooped down and clung to Picasso's shoulder. Three other people were in the same room. With only a laughing "How droll!" he cupped the silken creature in his hands and carried it back into the summer night.

Two snails were found creeping along the staircase balustrade. Picasso's first concern was, "They can't find food here. They'll starve!" So he caught them and bedded them down with fresh lettuce in a temporarily vacant bird cage in the dining room. Each Sunday he took them out to sprinkle water into their shells. "Maybe they'll think it's rain."

There was an aloof screech owl who lived on an unused potter's wheel in the studio. Only burning stares greeted anyone other than Picasso. For him he clicked his beak in a cheery, brittle way and did a curtsying dance on his perch until the Maestro let him sit on his finger. Baby pigeons on the third-floor balcony did nothing whatsoever when Jacqueline or any of the others of us were near. The moment Picasso appeared they went almost crazy, fluttering naked wings, trying to walk, and gurgling deep in their scrawny, unkempt bodies. Picasso petted and cuddled those miserable fledglings into thinking he really was their mother.

One morning, alone in the studio, I watched a slowly pulsating white butterfly float through the sunlight of the open garden doors. It flew without hesitation into all of the rooms. There was no frenzied beating of wings against the great glass windows. After a few minutes of casual looking around, it flew out again. It seemed as much at home in the studio as in the garden.

Maybe it was a reflection of this enormous sensitivity to nature and love of all life that was the key to Picasso's feelings for his pictures. He was the father *and* the mother of his canvases. While they remained nothing more than naked paint they could still receive whatever nourishment he might offer through his brush. Their metamorphosis was not complete. Once framed they were on their own. The umbilical cord was cut. The Maestro turned to something else.

Near the ceramics village of Vallauris, on a hilltop above Cannes, there was an almost forgotten generation of these easel offspring that had never been completely severed from the Maestro. They waited patiently in his once bustling but now abandoned studio. He had left the place nearly four years ago—by simply walking out and locking the doors. Everything remained rigidly in its niche. Nothing was moved, dusted, sold or looked at again. One afternoon, leaving Lump and Yan to hold down *La Californie,* Picasso abruptly loaded Jacqueline, Sabartés, Frelaut, Kathy, Martine and me into Janot's nine-seater Citroen—and away we went to visit "the old neighborhood."

Picasso led the way, finding keys for padlocks rusting on their hasps. The deeper we went, the less it was an artist's studio. Heavy, moldering air muted every voice. Little light penetrated its depths. Most of the doors remained closed. Whatever illumination there was sneaked in past the few flimsily barred windows that had never been shuttered. But in those places where light did shine, one felt as if he were discovering the catacombed temple of a fabled but long-lost tribe. Grotesque masks and spidery idols stood on rough altars. A chiseled goat's head—of unknown ritualistic significance—stood impaled on a pole, stark and sacrificed. An innocent sprite hovered in space . . . contrived of wicker baskets and twisted rope, her flowing curls only corrugated paper, cast in plaster. Finally, hooded with darkness, there was an innermost sanctuary. If Picasso's pagans had a priestess, this was her court. Its walls were encrusted with crenellated urns and miniature birds such as were left behind by the Pharaohs' priests when they sealed their pyramids along the Nile. Ever-watchful sirens — some moon-eyed, others suspicious — guarded the place, for their priestess was but a sultry girl with an owl for her pet. She was nude and sensuous . . . and stretching at that very moment to rise from her bath.

I asked Picasso about her, for she was like no work of his I had ever seen. "Oh," he replied. "You mean 'La Gazelle'?" I said that I had no idea what it was named but I meant the rapturous nude, which might have been an Etruscan wall painting. "Yes, yes, that's it! That's 'La Gazelle'." Never before had I heard of Picasso's naming anything he painted. It was always done by others long after he had finished. For him to have called that girl "The Gazelle"—for the delicate and extremely elusive African antelope—surprised me completely. I said so. Picasso exploded with laughter, his brown-black eyes shining with merriment as he answered. "Look, Gypsy. Stop dreaming! Gazelle is just a name given by ceramists to the clay pipes used as dish racks in the kiln. They keep new plates from sticking together or falling in the fire. That's what she's painted on."

Kathy and Martine were realists, too. Both had hurried through the studio to spend the rest of the afternoon in the kiln rooms with Jules Agar, Picasso's potter. They stood tirelessly before his wheel as he molded cups and vases by the dozens . . . from plain clods of clay.

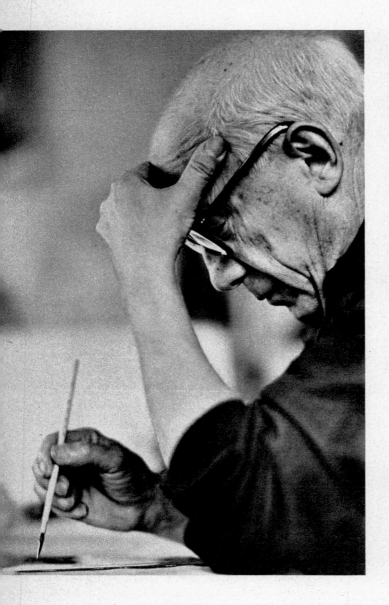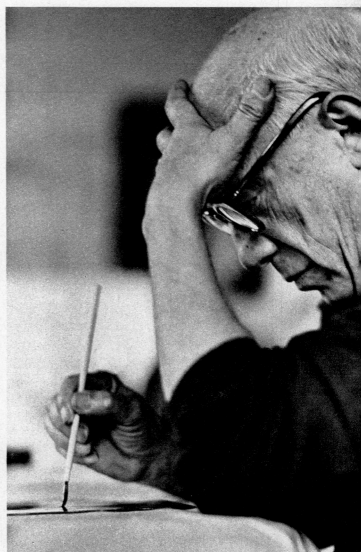

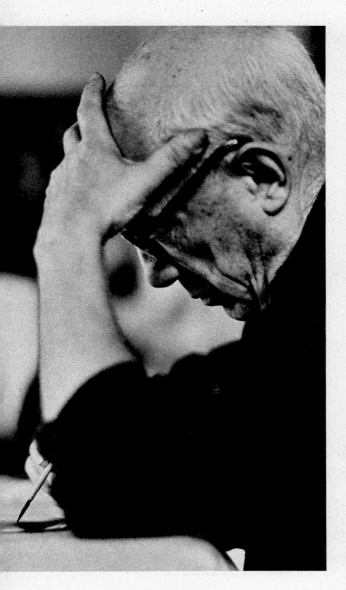

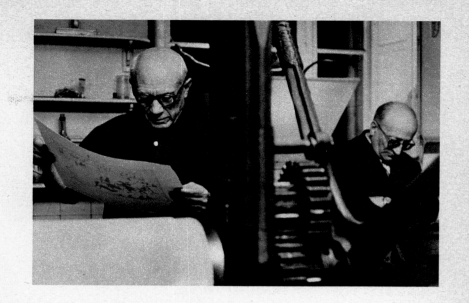

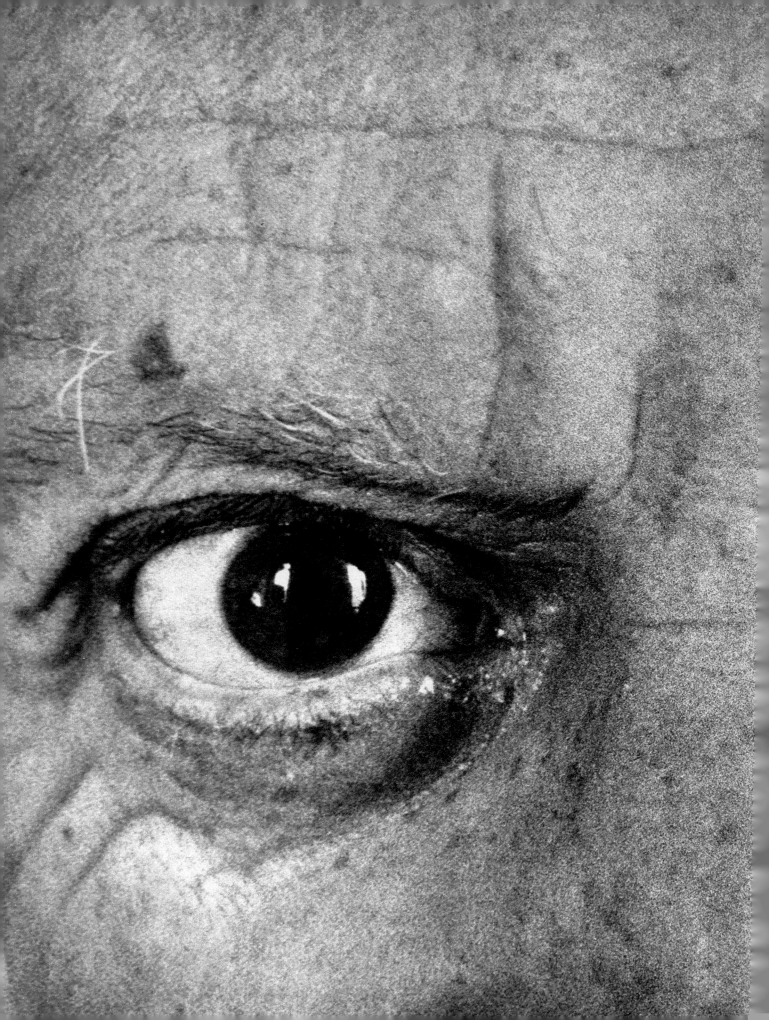

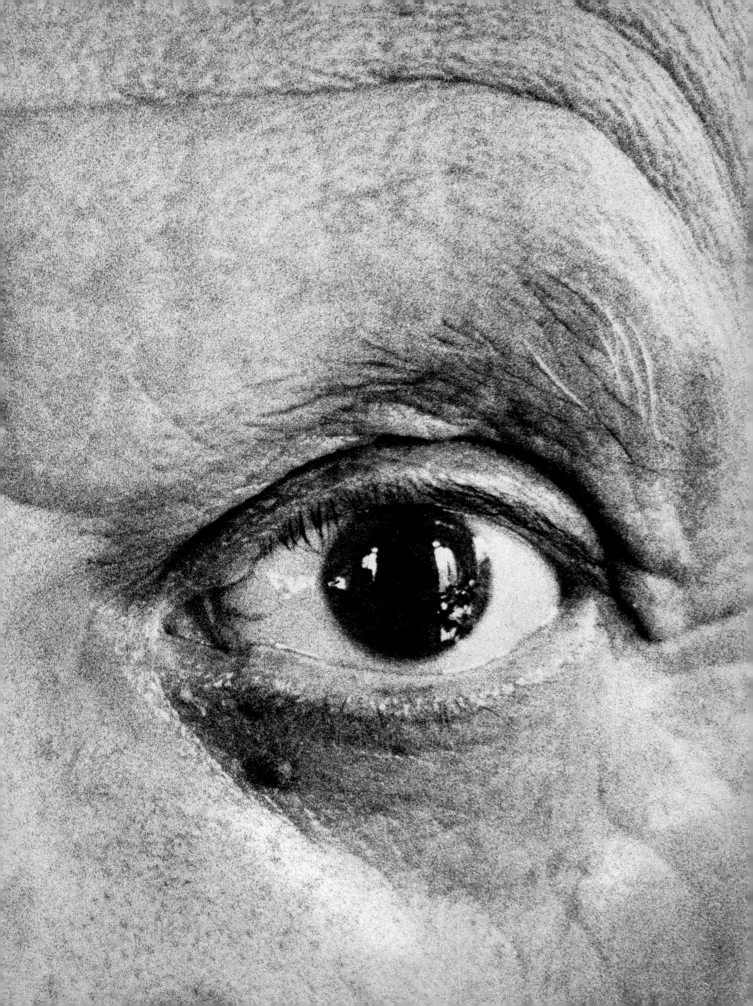

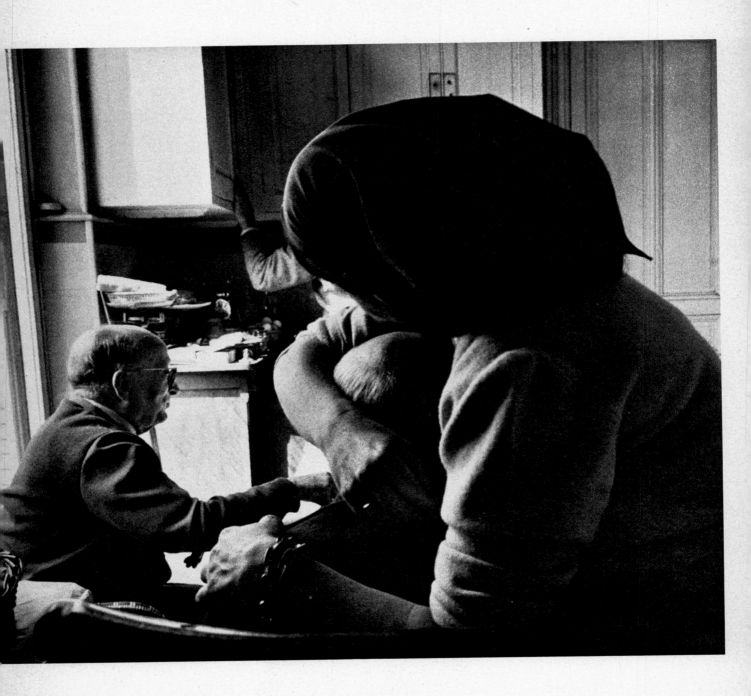

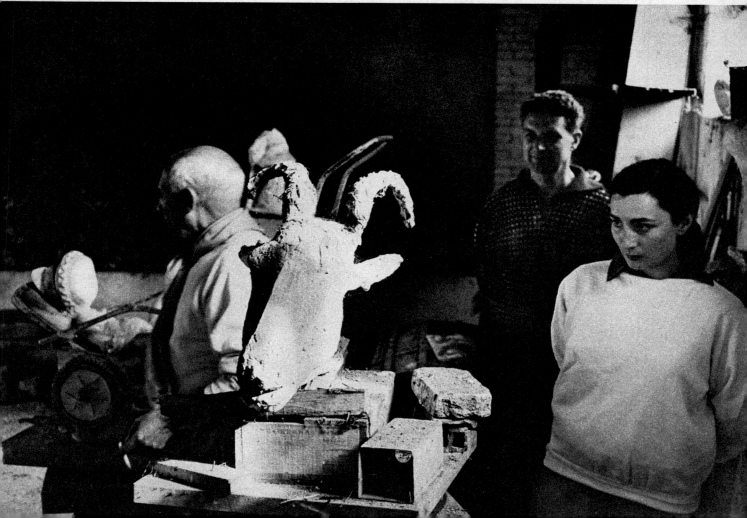

Spring soon vanished. Picasso's week-after-week activities had kept exploding in so many different directions that more than 5,000 negatives sped through my cameras, yet I still saw fresh picture opportunities everywhere. They were a continuing source of amazement to me, because nearly all of the action took place within the same three rooms of the studio or in the garden. Even so the story seemed destined to run into eternity. A cablegram finally forced the visit to an end; I must fly to the United States without delay. Though I had no photographs of Picasso actually painting on canvas—something he had ignored for over half a year—I knew that I had more than enough of everything else about *La Californie* to publish quite a book. When I told Picasso and Jacqueline that I had to leave, that all was finished, Picasso answered simply, "You know best. You know your work. But remember! This is your house." As I intended returning home to Italy through Cannes, I parked my racing Mercedes-Benz in his garage . . . after getting his promise not to touch it. His first, and last, experiment in piloting Jacqueline's little car had ended with devastated flowerbeds, an uprooted tree and his joyous discovery of a world he had never explored.

It was midsummer before I got back. I was thrilled to find Picasso with the entire family and some friends at the airport. They had brought Lump, to see if he still knew me. The Maestro was drably outfitted in a bright lemon shirt and plain red slacks. Lump had matured in his company. He didn't wee-wee at all, despite his frenzied excitement when he recognized me. I had come back only to say good-by, then pick up my car and head for home. But when I walked into the studio I saw what I had half expected—the place had changed. The Maestro still worked a bit on the dinner table while Jacqueline clipped reports of his exhibitions for her scrapbooks, but someone had tried to clear the floors, all of the ceramics were gone, and several unknown pictures stood on the easels . . . Picasso had really begun to paint. Instead of saying "adiós" I got out my cameras and stayed for another six weeks.

Summertime was tourist time in Cannes. They came from all over the world to lie in the sun or to skin-dive off the Côte d'Azur. Many of them tried to see Picasso. Some found his phone number. Very few got into the villa. There just was no time. As the Maestro once lamented, "Time! That's the thing. When it's gone, it's gone. No argument! Like a taxi meter ticking over."

For some friends, of course, the door was always open even though it disrupted his work schedule. One was Gary Cooper. They had met the year before when Gary brought his family to the Riviera after finishing a movie in Paris. They got along fine. Picasso juggled English words remembered from Thanksgiving dinners in the Paris apartment of Gertrude Stein—around 1905—and Cooper gingerly unlimbered the Spanish he remembered from "For Whom the Bell Tolls"—released in 1943. "Rocky," Gary's wife, handled French fairly well and Jacqueline's English, while hesitant, was sound. But Picasso and Cooper would have no part of anything but fast-drawing whatever words came to them first, with nobody standing in-between.

Cooper brought the Maestro two great gifts. One was the ten-gallon white Stetson he had worn in "Saratoga Trunk." The hat got immediate top-billing in Picasso's wardrobe. The other present was a Colt .45, a frontier-style sidearm. Cooper also managed to find a handful of cartridges in his pocket. Picasso took one look, flipped his new sombrero toward a lampshade and stalked, stiff-legged, into the garden—pistol in one hand, an empty paint can in the other. Reassuring everyone that the chief of police was a friend of his, "Don't worry! Don't worry!," he and Gary started shooting it out against one of the palm trees. Jacqueline, Rocky, Maria—the Coopers' art-student daughter—Kathy and Lump hurriedly searched for foxholes. The two gunmen blasted flaming lead into the dusk. Bark and sand flew everywhere. The slumbering pigeons on the balcony above took off. With the last shot gone Picasso stood flint-eyed, blowing smoke from the barrel. Cooper could be heard muttering, "It's a heck of a lot easier in the movies!" The can was absolutely intact.

Probably only Lucas Cranach, the witty fifteenth-century German painter, could have fully appreciated the delightful satire of his "Venus and Amour," which the Maestro had turned out in gouache one day in June. It was on the easel in the dining room when I returned from the States. Venus was seen standing stark naked, except for a diaphanous veil held mincingly in front of her hips. An enormous picture hat and two looping necklaces of jewels of questionable quality completed her attire. Expressionless mouse-eyes bulged from a disproportionately tiny, bird-pecked apple of a face. Amour stood beside her in the form of Cupid holding a honeycomb which he had just swiped from a nearby tree in the forest where they were rendezvousing. Naturally, the bees were stinging him, and he was in tears. It was a very funny painting . . . also profound. It formed a backdrop for Jacqueline's and Picasso's after-lunch moments when there were no visitors and they just talked.

Cooper's white Stetson became a conspicuous addition to the household. The Maestro wore it constantly. With it on he became inquisitive about America. He had told me earlier that he had wanted to visit America when he was young but could never afford it. Then, when he could easily have met any expense, he was too busy. He was excited by what I recalled from roaming through Texas and Arizona and California. I told him of arid, wind-swept ranches and of the taciturn, leathery men who lived there . . . for they were like Spain, and Spaniards. "Yes, yes," he would reply, "I knew Americans like that. In Paris, years ago. Not fancy, like now. They finished meat bones with their hands. Men! Like Cooper! Wild ones like Hemingway, too. But they never came back." Jacqueline said she wanted to see Arizona. "Yes, yes. We'll go!" Picasso would enthuse. "In a wagon. With a donkey. With Lump. Slowly. Then we'll see the land."

Picasso had a fairly accurate knowledge of American history around the turn of the century. I was perplexed until one day Jacqueline's dropping sugar into her coffee provided the answer. Picasso had broken the cube for her. As he handed her half he turned to me with a slow grin and asked whether Yankee sugar companies still controlled Cuba—as in the days of "Muceenlee" and the "Maan." I was utterly lost for a moment—then floored. He was referring to President

William McKinley and the United States battleship *Maine* . . . to the Spanish-American War.

Another day I was dumbfounded when he abruptly burst into song. With the very first stanza Jacqueline fled, hands over her ears. He had pushed back his chair and begun chanting ribald parodies of Mexican tunes, ending with a real horror based on ''La Cucaracha.'' He apparently remembered every line. He had learned them from Mexican painters in Paris, fifty years before. After Jacqueline returned he confessed, ''That's all they taught me.''

Following the Coopers' visit Picasso often flourished the empty Colt while entertaining guests, just as he had worn the clown's mask earlier in the year. A French-speaking Russian art expert, Michel Alpatov, arrived from Moscow and Picasso gave him a flashing lesson in pistolmanship that would have staggered even Gary. He then led him on a tour of the studio which ended in front of the Picasso-Cranach ''Venus.'' Coming as he had from a country where pictures were painted within clearly dictated limitations—or not at all—it was hardly surprising that the Russian stood benumbed by the casual way the Maestro had whipped him through the freest studio known to modern art.

After Alpatov had gone Picasso turned to me and said, ''I saw you dodging when we had the pistol out. Don't worry! I carried one in Paris years ago. I know how to handle them!'' Naturally I asked if he had carried one because of bandits. That really shook him. ''Bandits! Rob *us!* We didn't even have bread! Bandits! I just liked the noise, and sometimes it was stuffy in the studio so we shot holes in the ceiling. Once we shot holes in the roof of a carriage, too, then jumped out the other side and ran around in time to go back in with the police—looking for the vandals. Really, we were very young!''

My own introduction to an unforgettable experience was provided one day by an Italian artist who painted in Padua—nearly 600 years ago. His name was Guariento. I had found an altar panel of his in London, showing St. Michael weighing earthlings' souls at the gates of Paradise. After several years' delay I was taking it home to add to my small collection of paintings. I mentioned it at lunch and Picasso immediately wanted to see it. After studying it he turned and asked if I would like to see another early religious picture. I had always heard that he had Cézannes and Gauguins, Modiglianis and Matisses, but never realized his collection included church art. First, he unlocked a cabinet in the studio and returned with a leather folio. Paper-clipped to the cover was a snapshot of a child and a sleek, strangely familiar, man. I should have sensed what was coming when he leaned over my shoulder and added, ''That's Paolo, my son, when he was little—and that's Rudolph Valentino.''

Then he flipped open the folio. A packet of papers fell out. He started to read one. I unfolded another. It was a letter composed like a miniature newspaper, dated September 15, '94, edited and illustrated by a journalist named Pablo Ruiz. I looked carefully at others. Some were dated '92, some '91. Two, even more wrinkled than the rest, were just pages from notebooks with no dates or signatures at all. They were the oldest—from 1888 or '89. They were drawings showing Cervantes' Don Quixote and Sancho Panza as knights. There were other drawings of arguing women, thieving ruffians, doves and rabbits and fighting bulls, soldiers, village elders and city dandies, an old woman sewing, and a newsboy in the rain. There was one sketch of a stubby, bespectacled gentleman who could have been Toulouse-Lautrec, but the words below identified him only as ''a father of family.'' Finally I came to a fat turkey under which ran the line, ''To the hero of Christmas.'' It was the cover design on Editor Ruiz' issue for December 25, 1895. Inside was a drawing of Christ giving grace to the Devil at His feet. There was no caption. The casually bundled parcel held the earliest souvenirs—which were also the earliest unpublished work—of a child born in 1881, soon to become known simply as ''Picasso'' to the world of his time . . . maybe forever.

La Californie's greatest change that summer was in Picasso's shifting his work from the dinner table to the room across the house which once had been the villa's library. He owned thousands of books but kept them crated and stored in the attic. He read few new ones aside from those dealing with his own or other painters' work. He had no intention of racking these upon the walls ''like stuffed animals after the chase.'' His library lay on the floors or tables—wherever he first unwrapped them—or around his bed. So, the library became his studio. It flouted the classical law that an artist's studio must be built around uniformly diffused north light. Direct sunlight poured into that room through its unshuttered windows—from the south. Since Picasso started painting in the afternoons and continued far into the night under floodlights, it made little difference. Besides, most of his subjects were posing in his head, where the light never varied.

It was in that library-studio, after returning from America, that I saw Picasso's newest paintings. For the first time since arriving at the villa I was over my artistic depth. I had admired the bullfight aquatints, the eagles and owls on the plate series, and even enjoyed the most extreme of the bronzes around the doors and in the garden. On the latest paintings I foundered. I started searching for a key to unlock any door that might lead to understanding those strange people who had arrived amongst us at *La Californie*.

I compared Picasso's work to that of a physicist whose mathematical equations I could never solve for lack of higher education in that field but a few of whose symbols I could smugly recognize, remembered from days in college. Then I considered my inability to read much of the score of a great opera—although I could hum the arias because the music was so popular. Next I turned to alphabets like the Siamese and the Arabic in which I once could falteringly—but delightedly— piece together a couple of words learned while wandering around the world. I came back to the Maestro. Perhaps I found his works disturbing, possibly even resented them, because unlike mathematics or music or alphabets where combinations of graphic signs only formed inanimate patterns reflecting our civilization, he was using Man's physical features themselves to form human equations such as had never walked the face of our earth.

Then one night we were sitting on the garden steps. Stars were piled upon stars until they had lost all patterns—and I found my key!

I remembered other nights, many years before, when I had sailed the Mosquito Coast of Central America aboard the fastest schooner in the Caribbean. Powered only by canvas, she was more than a hundred feet long and was manned by a crew of eleven Cayman Islanders. They were

continued on page 157

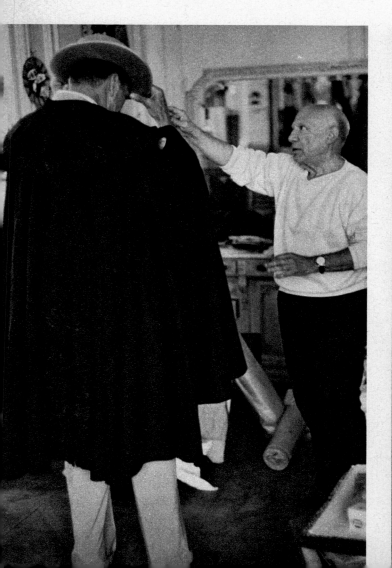

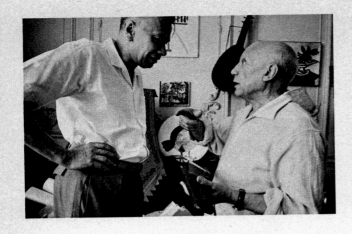 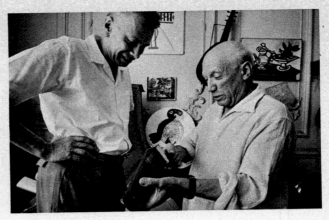

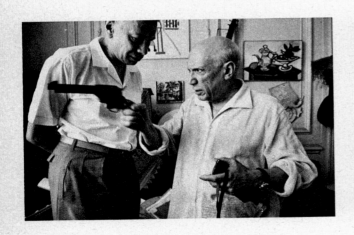 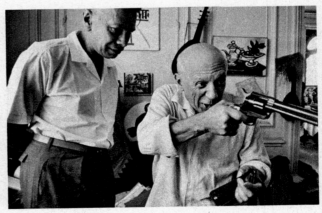

Dos Barbianas.

aventura dell caballero de los espejos

vededor de periodicos.

Un vededor de periodicos.

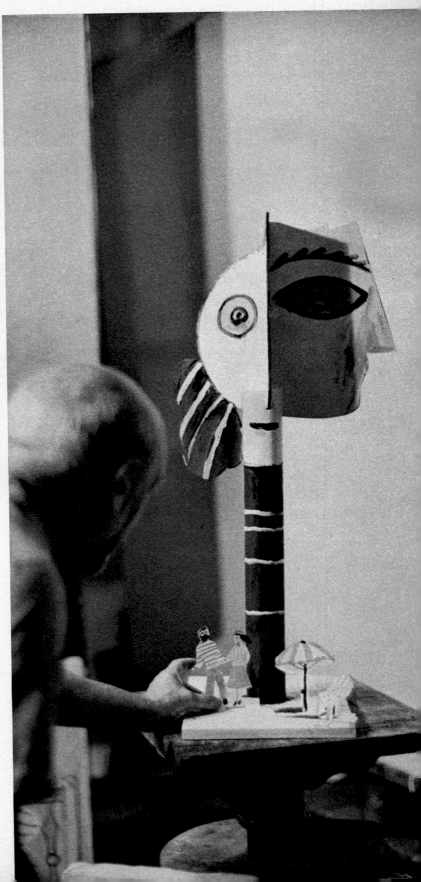

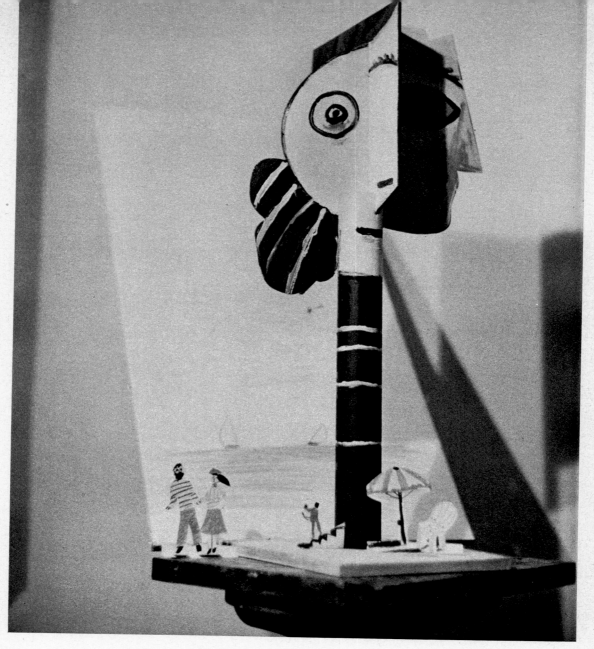

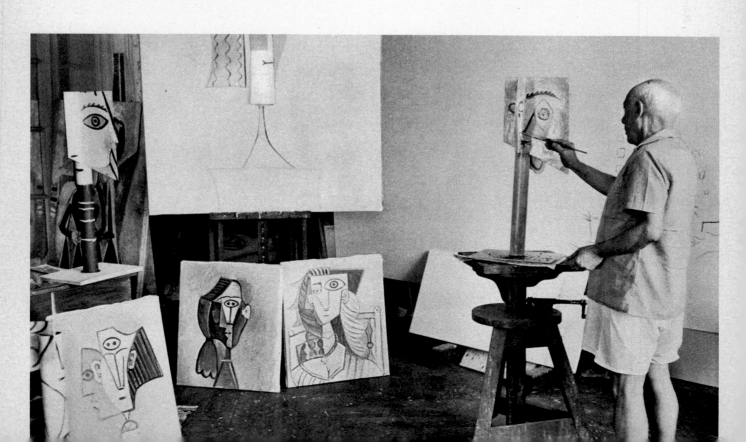

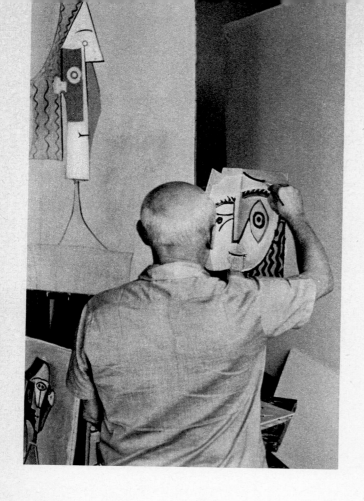
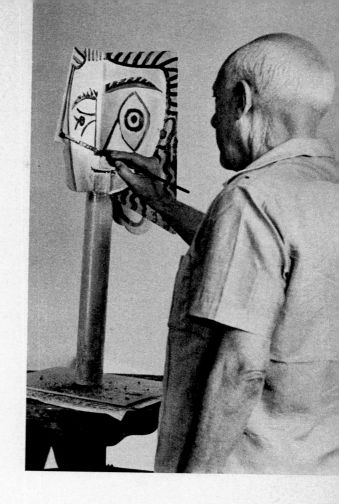

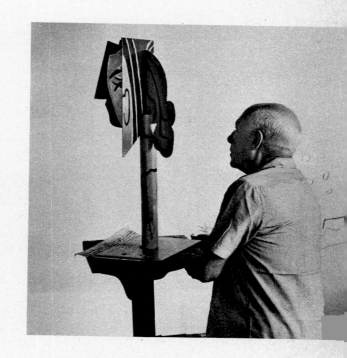

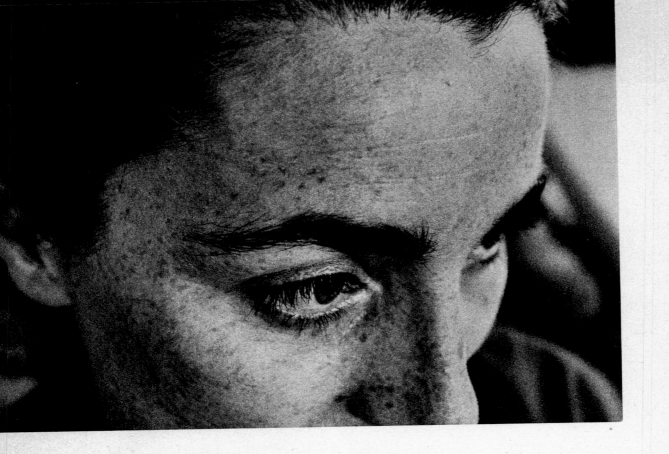

148

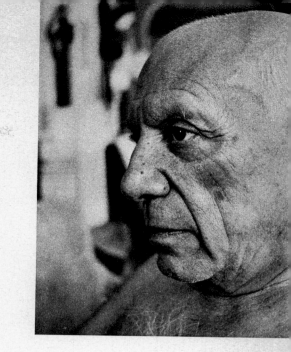

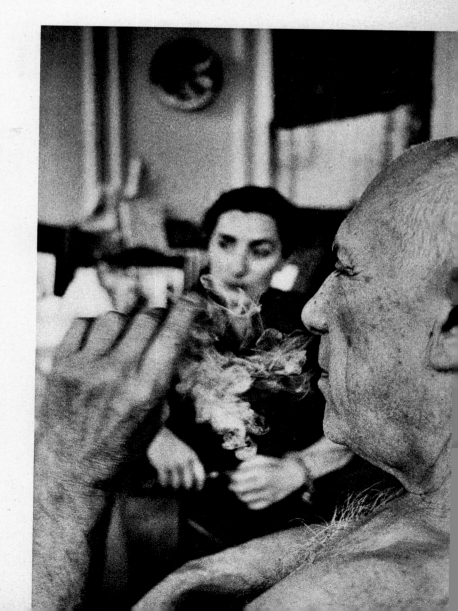

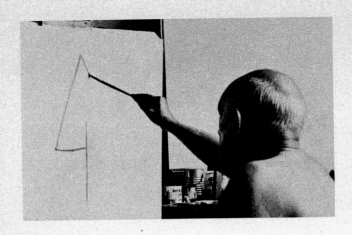
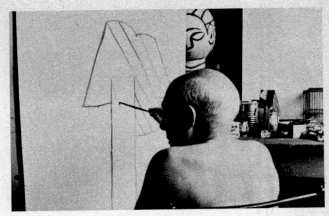

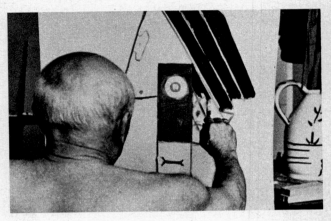

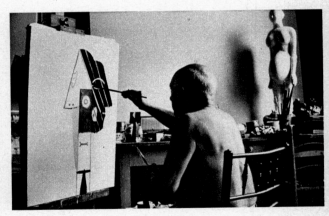
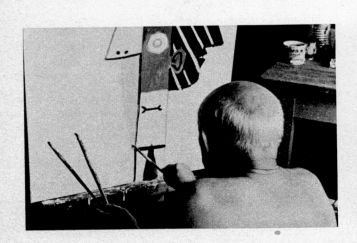
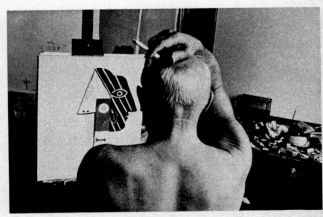

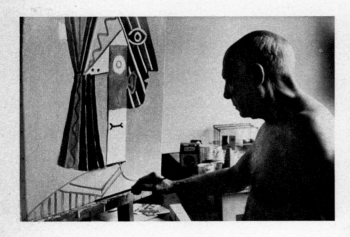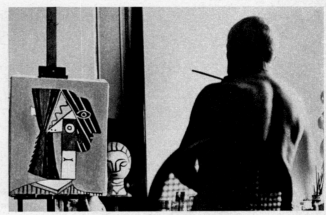
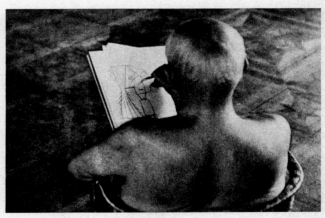

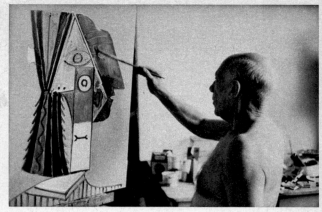
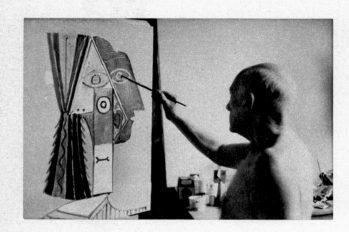
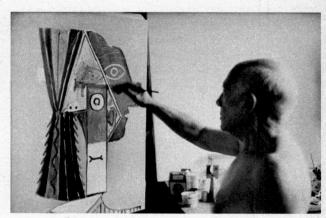
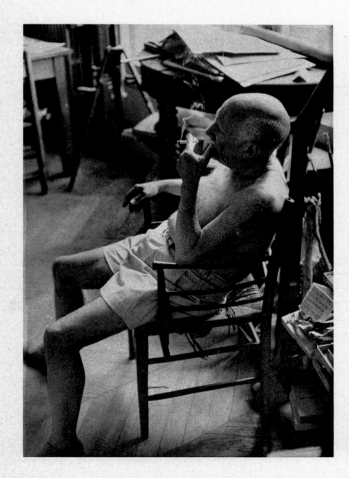

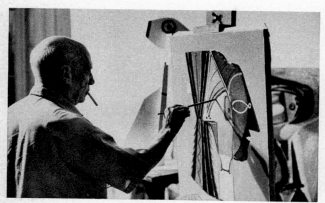

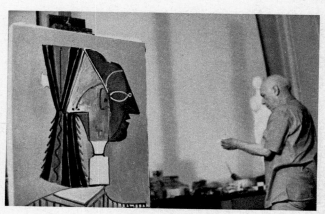

among the toughest sailors and finest navigators in the world. Their captain was a salt-saturated block of a man named Allie Ebanks, who never swore, conducted church services on the afterdeck Sunday mornings and literally beat that great vessel through the reefs along the Nicaraguan shore with his bare hands—at night.

The sky meant many things to Captain Ebanks. The stars even more. We often sat together on the cabin roof while he smoked his pipe and navigated us through the night. The voyage lasted nearly two months . . . two months of nights, when he tried to show me what it was that he saw far above our masts. For him the night sky was full of friends. The Great Bear and Cassiopeia and the Pleiades, all of the familiar constellations—and many more. They were celestial configurations which he knew at a glance, but for me they had to be traced out, night and night again. He started me on simple forms like the Dipper and Orion, but soon left me far behind. He saw turtles and whales and running horses, a pirate walking the plank, and even an angel. He saw their full figures very easily—among the same shot-gunned clusters of stars where I was blind. For him each was alive, and had enormous meaning. And that was absolutely all that mattered as he captained his own ship and charted his own course . . . to sail away across his sea.

Just as the studio had changed with summer, so Picasso had changed, too. He seemed caged. He paced the floor in his shorts. Cigarettes and sombreros and gaudy shirts made endless circles through his hands. Huge blank canvases lined the studio walls. He *really* was going back to work. Jacqueline stayed quietly with him, and always a little out of his way.

He started one evening after supper. He had paused beneath the floodlights, squinting at a three-dimensional, sheet-steel head of Jacqueline. It sat on his easel among the new paintings. It, too, was new. Jacqueline's neck was a vertically welded section of three-inch pipe. Picasso kept tunelessly whistling as he rotated the triple-flanged head under the lights, then, "Jacqueline! Es una cosa muy rara!"—"It is something very rare!" "Maybe, some day, people will live in houses like this—in the shaft itself—with the top for decoration."

Within minutes he had cut and colored cardboard figures of a honeymooning couple near their beach umbrella alongside the "house." A moment later he placed a doorman on the steps, then a feather-duster "palm tree" and a tiny globe of the world which, when scaled to the house, became a monument of colossal dimensions. He leaned an empty canvas behind the scene, sketching on it the Mediterranean horizon complete with sailboats. He noticed shadows of the steel-shafted sculpture. With charcoal he drew windows upon the shadows which to him had appeared as "old-fashioned" hotels along the beach behind his new house. He kept repeating, "Sí. Es una cosa muy rara!" Within fifteen minutes he had imagined and created another world. When he sat back with Jacqueline, laughing about the whole thing, I suddenly saw the truth of the sculpture's steel profile when compared to that of the girl herself. They were the same.

All that remained of the fantasy when Picasso opened the studio next day were the cardboard cutouts, the steel statue, the feather duster and the charcoal marks on the canvas. The magic of the shadow-house was gone. The Maestro soon had the easel cleared and another blank steel head before him. He immediately painted full face, profile, and fragments of both on the flanges of metal. By rotating the head, many different aspects of the same portrait became visible. Sculpture was one of man's most ancient means of self-expression—but he had added something provocative, and new.

During those infrequent occasions when Picasso sat smoking, doing nothing but thinking, the silence within his studio gave the rest of the villa a voice of its own . . . the faintest twittering of the screech owl who sat daydreaming on his perch . . . Lump's collar tags tinkling together when he turned to watch a fly . . . Kathy's laughter far away in the garden where she played with Martine . . . the almost imperceptible, slowly measured, woosh-woosh-woosh as Picasso shuffled his Moroccan slippers a few inches back and forth on the floor. Then he would be up and gone, dragging into the studio wood-and-cardboard knock-togethers, which just as quickly disappeared from view. They were ripples on the surface of his thinking—only he knew what went on below. He had assembled an entire wall full of these cardboard creatures one afternoon, then shoved them aside after a single over-all glance, when he brought a canvas from the front of the house and began to paint. Without a word . . . without dramatics . . . with just a single, sweeping, straight line of black paint on white canvas Pablo Picasso started painting in his own studio under the eye of a camera: the most impregnable taboo in modern art lay shattered.

Picasso was totally relaxed as he painted. He looked as though he had been seated in front of his easel forever—and might be there forevermore. He built his painting—a portrait of Jacqueline—upon surprisingly simple, but solid, geometrical foundations of structural lineal supports, just as an engineer welds structural steel girders into the skeleton for a skyscraper. Both were intended to stand for a long time. There was no haste, no uncertainty, when he painted—as there had been none when he etched the bullfight aquatints, earlier in the year. He started to paint in mid-afternoon, and worked until midnight. He stopped only once, to cook an omelette for Jacqueline's and his own supper, then returned immediately to his easel. As the hours passed, he created, then painted over, at least three powerfully complete pictures. After one of these had appeared, and vanished, he turned and dryly observed, "Now, you see that it's really not easy—and it's much, much easier to start than to stop!"

Portrait eyes came and went. So did ears and mouths and profiles, and hair scarfs, and latticed shadows falling harshly across Jacqueline's head. To me, it was never the Jacqueline I had seen around the villa. But I thought of Captain Ebanks on his schooner at night. I accepted, equally, Picasso's way of finding his favorite stars, and of tracing myriad figures while navigating through *his* night. He was sailing into waters where no one had gone before him. Although he twisted and turned and changed sails many times to pass the reefs he saw ahead, he was free to chart his own course, in his own ship . . . out across his sea.

For weeks the painting remained in the studio exactly the way it was that night when the Maestro finally turned away, wiping off his brushes. Then one morning I saw that it had changed. During the night Picasso had swept away its entire profile. Apparently the picture was off on another voyage after having been becalmed.

That was the day I asked one of my few questions. I had always wanted to know which was his favorite among all of the so-called "Periods" of his career—Blue . . . Rose . . . Cubist . . . Realist —which one? He was hugging Jacqueline, for she had just seen what he had done to her portrait. He looked up at me with his eyes really glowing and answered, "The next one."

Very few men recognized the significance of the unknown Spaniard's revolutionary style of painting earlier than a young Paris art merchant named Daniel-Henry Kahnweiler. He became the Maestro's dealer in 1907. During the next half-century hundreds of Picasso's pictures went through his hands. He established a worldwide network of sub-dealers to whom he rationed Picassos somewhat as the DeBeers diamond syndicate rations the flow of gems. Picasso's production was treated as something equally rare—and nearly as expensive. Kahnweiler became an authority on modern art . . . and a millionaire, too.

It was during one of Kahnweiler's visits that bursts of laughter brought Picasso and Jacqueline rushing from the house and into the arms of his youngest son and daughter, Claude and Paloma. The two had just arrived from Paris where they lived with their mother, who had left the artist when they were babies. Holidays were still spent with their father. Immediately all work stopped. *La Californie* became a gymnasium, and a theater—run for children.

Claude, ten, found the white Stetson. Then, with a blaring bugle, he accompanied his eight-year-old sister in an Apache war dance around the dinner table. Paloma burrowed under a chair and jumped up wearing Picasso's clown disguise. Claude found another clown's costume, and a flute —which lured Picasso from behind his canvases to be the assistant. For other wild minutes the boy and the Maestro scuffled all over the studio floor, boxing. The 10-year-old threw long right hooks which the 75-year-old deftly blocked, his eyes wrinkling with pride.

Picnics were organized to nearby beaches. Other days, while Kathy and Claude raced their bicycles around the driveway, Paloma stayed at the table after lunch. She was copying her father's paintings lining the walls. Then she drew Spanish galleons and clusters of wild flowers and portraits of everyone in the house. She tugged leaves from bushes and fingernail-cut them into puppets with startled eyes and pouting mouths. It was Paloma who poked happy faces into her ice cream before it melted. While Picasso gouged out linoleum for lithographs, she continued working right beside him. They treated each other as equals—without questions, advice or criticism. Seeing them together, I kept thinking that in another generation a girl might become the reigning artist of the world, and that it could be Paloma—Picasso's daughter.

Evenings were warm, so the entire family moved out onto the garden steps. Lump and the goat wandered freely, looking for something to eat. Jacqueline sat reading among the bronzes on the top step. Picasso stayed at the garden's edge on an old park bench, without saying a word. Once, after dark had fallen, he squeezed into a frightful rubber mask and tried to startle Paloma —who hugged herself with joy, then grabbed him painfully by the nose. His muffled "How droll!" echoed inside the mask as the children ran away to bed. Then he was out of the disguise and into a tasseled African cap . . . watching the mirror . . . lost in thought.

He disappeared into a studio corner and came back wearing an evil wig over a gaping, shark-mouthed, cardboard mask. His eyes glittered white-hot, fixed, and dangerous. He writhed before the mirror, his massive chest pumping in air until it seemed about to burst. Demoniac convulsions, like those of an equatorial witch doctor, racked him—and the mask was tossed aside. He rapidly cut out and put on another . . . of a mournful, thousand-year-old pelican. He scarcely moved. One reproachful eye watched from the face in the mirror, a face I had never seen before. Behind it my friend was hard at work.

The same night he hauled out a huge canvas that was splotched with ill-defined shapes. He started at the left margin with charcoal. Within ten minutes he was at the right and the whole thing was peopled by gawking Martian giants who joined the ranks of other curious characters along the studio walls. Picasso turned and said, "That's the beach at Garoupe—at least that's the way *I* see it!" Then he continued, "Other painters might spend a year going over every inch of a canvas. I've spent a year thinking about this one. Now, a few minutes' drawing—enough time to finish it!" Stepping back, he noticed his own shadow bending among the charcoal figures. Without another word he retrieved the pelican mask, then an ancient tripod. Fitted together they made a predatory, stilt-legged crab. Dissatisfied, he moved the contraption to one side of the canvas and started again, adding his clown's derby, a shirt and a guitar. The guitar was too much. Everything collapsed. Still without a word, he stuck the derby on his head and scraped the debris off the floor. The beach picture was to backdrop all studio activities for the rest of the summer.

Shortly thereafter, while at Garoupe with the children, two remarkable things happened. First, an enormous man arose from the water wearing a skin diver's underwater snorkel helmet pushed high upon his head. I knew that I had seen him somewhere before—then it hit me. He was the left-hand figure in Picasso's newest picture. Almost at the same time a boy came in to the beach on a paddle surfboard. As he approached us he swung the broad-bladed paddle across his chest— and *he* was the long-armed central figure in the same canvas. Picasso was right. The paddles were merely extensions of the boy's hands, letting him reach the water while riding the waves.

No individual day was ever better than any other at *La Californie*. They all seemed woven into a pattern of rich simplicity—the master design for one man's way of expressing himself, and for living, while on earth. There *were* several days, however, that seemed even gayer than others. One was when Picasso asked Jacqueline whether she remembered any ballet steps from school years. She did. Thereupon Picasso—barefoot and in swimming trunks—wanted to try them, too. After a fleeting minute's instructions he was twirling and thumping around the studio, mixing pirouettes and polkas and ponderous flippings and flappings of his own spontaneous invention. A house-shuddering finale of flailing arms and crashing feet ended his debut as a dancer. With only a "Well, now to work," he walked back toward his easel. At that moment Paloma and Claude came home from the beach. Jacqueline went to make sandwiches. Picasso bandaged a toe he had rammed against a chair while dancing. Then, sitting in his favorite old rocker, he devoted every thought to keeping time with Paloma while Claude skipped rope between them.

Watching them from across the studio floor . . . the boy leaping high into the air . . . the tense child and the silent man concentrating on a piece of rope and a game . . . the charcoal bathers of Garoupe assembled in the background . . . I realized that here was the heart of Picasso's greatness —and his finest message to men of his own or any other time. It had nothing to do with paint or canvas or bronze or charcoal or clay or colors, or material art in any form. It was just his daily, unspoken, exultant shout, "Es una cosa *muy* rara!," in answer to everyman's secret, wondering question about life itself.

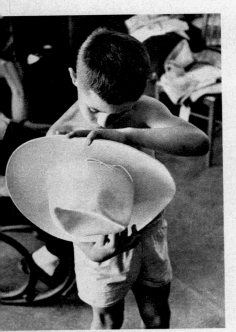

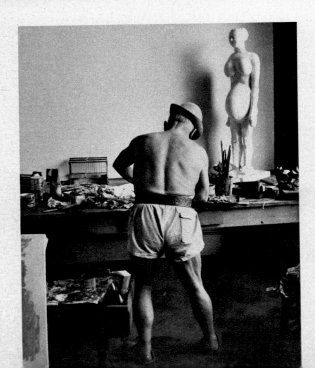

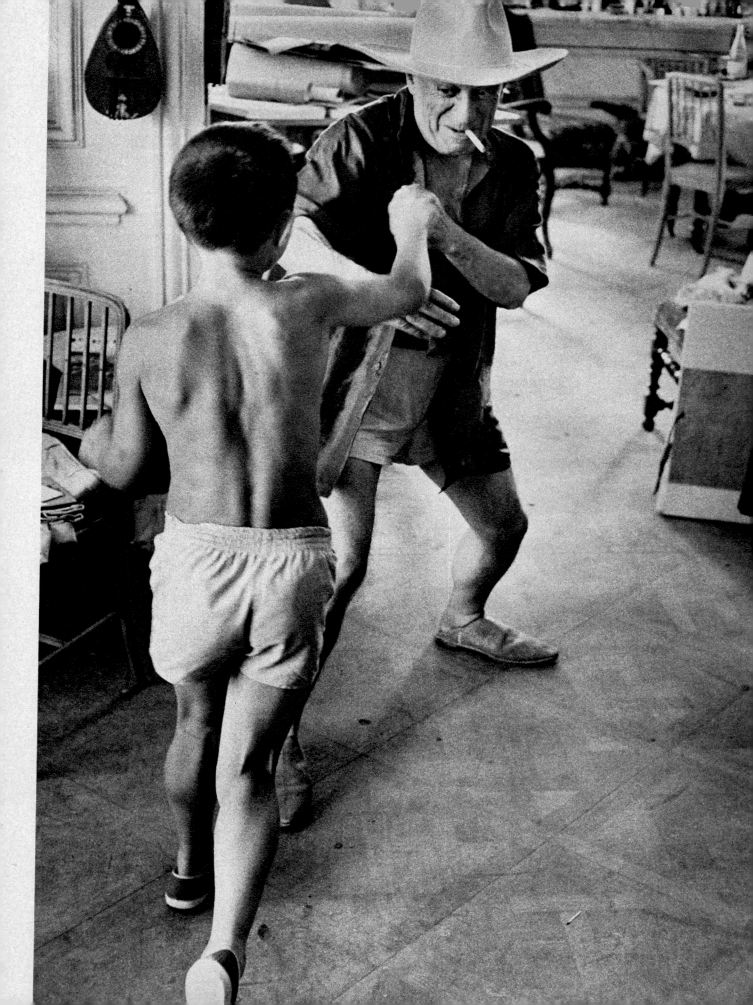

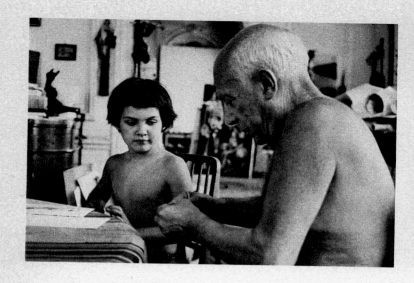

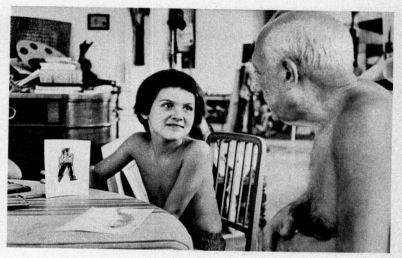

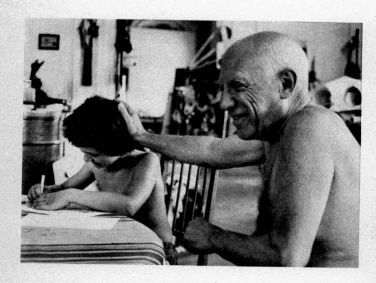

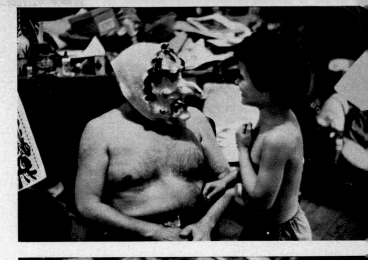

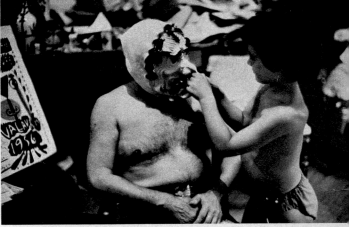

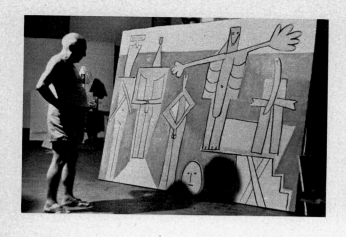

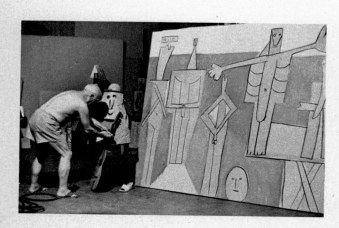

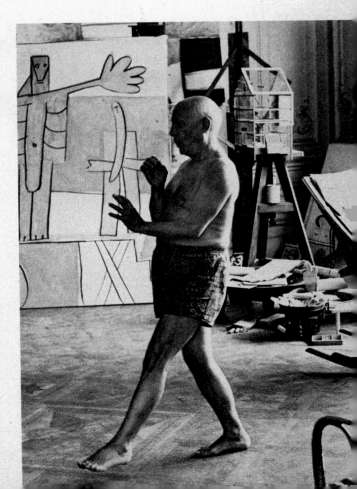

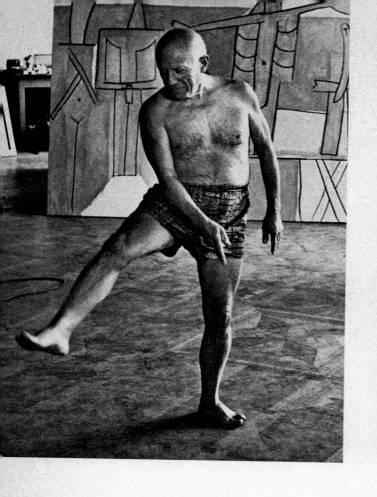

This book is dedicated to love.　　　　Este libro está dedicado al amor.

Ce livre est dédié à l'amour.　　　　愛にこの書をささぐ

اكرس هذا الكتاب للحب　　　　Questo libro è dedicato all'amore.

Dieses buch ist der liebe gewidmet.　　　　Эта книга посвящена любви.

此書是對愛的呈獻　　　　Denna bok är tillägnad kärleken.